EXERCISES IN THE 19th EDITION OF THE DEWEY DECIMAL CLASSIFICATION

About the Author

Mohinder Partap Satija, currently a Professor in Library and Information Science in the Guru Nanak Dev University, is in the library profession for the last 30 years. As an author of more than a dozen books and about 100 papers published in Indian and foreign library journals, he has collaborated with international experts in India and abroad. He has visited Germany, France, Finland, England, Nepal, The Netherlands and Belgium in connection with professional work. He is associated with many library journals such as *Information Management Report* (Bowker-Saur, UK), *Library Times International* (USA), the *Lucknow Librarian* (India), *Ranganathan Research Bulletin* (India) and *Knowledge Organisation* (USA/Germany). He is the Indian Co-ordinator of the *International Society for Knowledge Organisation* (ISKO) (The Netherlands). Dr. Satija is a life member of many library and information science associations; and has delivered lectures in many universities. He served as a Visiting Fellow for three months in Maastricht McLuhan Institute, University of Maastricht in the summer of 1999, and is an advisor to the Harrod's Librarian's Glossary (Gower, UK).

EXERCISES IN THE 19th EDITION OF THE DEWEY DECIMAL CLASSIFICATION

M.P. SATIJA
Professor, Library and Information Science
Guru Nanak Dev University,
Amritsar

CONCEPT PUBLISHING COMPANY, NEW DELHI - 110059

ISBN 81-7022-878-6 (PB)

First Published 2001

Published and Printed by
Ashok Kumar Mittal
Concept Publishing Company
A/15-16, Commercial Block, Mohan Garden,
NEW DELHI - 110059

Phones: 5648039, 5649024
Fax : 091-11-5648053
E-Mail: publishing@conceptpub.com

Dedicated to
The Satinder Kaur Ramdev Memorial Trust
for
Advancement of Librarianship (SATKAL)
and its founder
S. Jaginder Singh Ramdev
First Deputy Librarian of Panjab University Library,
Chandigarh

PREFACE

A system of library classification that flashed across the inquiring mind of young Melvil Dewey on a fine May morning in 1873, is still the most popular one. Soon after its publication in 1876, its popularity fanned across the globe; the puck–like girdle that it put round the world is ever fastening. The sun never sets on its terrains. It is being used in 2,00,000 libraries in about 135 countries.

Historically speaking, the modern library classification begins with it. It provided a paradigm to all the library classification systems that have come up in its wake. Classification by discipline, depicting hierarchic relations, ingenious use of decimal notation and the relative index are its enduring contributions which have been borrowed by all the later classifications as their very basis. Some have improved over it in some ways but faltered in many more. None could catch up with its popularity, as a result. Despite the ever mounting criticism of its faulty approach and 19th century structure, its popularity has always shown a spiking graph. Not only this, the invention of the DDC played a vital role in giving a direction and shape to the modern librarianship. It is not for nothing Melvil Dewey is given the appellation of the father of modern librarianship!

Its revision is institutionalised and so is a continuous process. At present it is in its 21st edition (1996) and constantly keeps itself abreast of the ever advancing frontiers of knowledge to cater to the increasing demand of its users. In every revision, it has been expanded, modified, rectified and made more modern in methods by applying the results of the latest research in library classification. Since Melvil Dewey (1851-1931), it has come a long way in its endeavours to meet the needs of the society overwhelmed by the information revolution. It has been translated in about 35 major languages of the world ranging from Vietnamese, Hebrew, Arabic, Hindi and Thai to French German and Italian. In many countries, its relevant portions have been recast and expanded to suit their local needs to offset its western, Anglo-Saxon and Protestant WASPish bias. Some of such adaptations and home-made expansions are officially recognised

Yet many librarians criticize it for its enumerative pattern. The criticism is now only partially valid. It is getting faceted edition by edition. They plead to abandon it or not to adopt it but fail to provide a better alternative. Frustrated, they declare classification as an impossibility or absurdity. They throw away the baby with the water bath! Many a storm have raged over to uproot it. Always it has come out unscathed. At times, it was forsaken by some to be readopted later. Deserters had to come back to its fold eventually. Once declared dead, it is now pulsating with a vigorous life. It is living and kicking and is a very influential system in many ways. The system is well poised to play its role in the information society of the 21st century, both in print and electronic version.

Notwithstanding the fashion to criticize it, the system has become the very marrow in the bones that a librarian make. It has become an institution of librarianship as it now more or less involves the whole community of librarians in its making. It is the only gateway to learn the theory and practice of library classification; and for many it is the end. For many others, the DDC means the classification.

One of the repeated and much dinned about charge is that having no philosophy of its own, it is not based on any theory. In a sense, it is true and admitted with a candour. True to the spirit of the times and the country of its origin, Melvil Dewey, imbued with pragmatism and business-sense, never allowed to sacrifice utility over the cold philosophy and hair-splitting academics. His was a practical scheme that squarely answered the basic problems of classifying and arranging books in the U.S. libraries.

Despite its professed practical nature, it has over the years given rise to many interesting and revealing theoretical studies. A good part of total classification literature is exclusively devoted to this system. It invariably constitutes a central chapter on any book on general classification. Tide of literature on DDC is constantly swelling. Some of its studies have shed searching light on the socio-politico-cultural bearings of classification. It has been a subject of some doctoral dissertations, research reports and experiments. Many studies have been made to study its use in online databases. It is a pioneer system to make effective use of information technology in its editing and production.

The scheme as a practical classification is taught in all the library schools in India and the world over. But due to some unexplained reasons, not many textbooks elucidating the ever becoming complex process of number building have appeared in proportionate measure of its popularity. This is more true of DDC-19. There are not many standard sets of exercises to teach the rudiments and illustrate the synthesis of class numbers in a graded way. Perhaps it is thought too simple and obvious to the students. forgetting that still waters run deep. Consequently many finer beauties and versabilities remain uncovered to the students. And as a result of this erroneous thought or due to some otherwise inherent difficulties, our library literature is rarefied in this area. It is, however, not to ignore the books that have been published on the subject:

Bloomberg, Marty and Weber, Hans: *An introduction to classification and number building in Dewey.*
Littleton, Colo: Libraries Unlimited, 1976.
Batty, C.D.: *An introduction to the nineteenth edition of the Dewey Decimal Classification.* London: Clive Bingley, 1981.
Osborne, Jeanne: *Dewey Decimal Classification, 19th edition: a study manual,* Littleton, Colo: Libraries Unlimited, 1982
Gangadhara Rao, P: *Synthesis in DDC 18th edition.*
Waltair: Andhra University Press, 1983.
Dhyani, Pushpa: *Dhyani's Guide to Dewey Decimal Classification.*
New Delhi: Metropolitan Book Co., 1985.

The present book simply aims to introduce the students to the process of assigning and especially synthesising the class numbers by the 19th edition of the DDC. The book is student-oriented and only aims at them. The chapters and the examples have been graded to some extent. No background, whatsoever, has been assumed on the part of the users. Though, it aims at the beginner, yet it provides a complete course to train the students in the techniques of subject analysis and number building involving the use of various auxiliary tables and multiple synthesis. The graded process of number building may mirror before the students the increasing faceted nature of the system and its advancing steps towards, what S R Ranganathan terms as, depth classification. To avoid verbosity the number building has been depicted through equations and facet formulae. It may mentally stimulate the students. It is hoped that in this play-way fashion the students will learn the ropes of the DDC through this how-to-do-it text.

The examples, chosen of necessity, are largely imaginary though not far from the realities of the literary warrant. The aim is to be amply illustrative and to step-by-step introduce the new concepts and methods.

In the process some repetition is inevitable, for which the forbearance of the readers is sought. Another aim is to be simple and clear. It is admitted that to write simply here has been as simple and difficult as to write on "how to lace a shoe." The obvious things make it difficult to write on.

The text is based on the 19th edition of the DDC. But it is hoped that the students using the DDC-18 will find no difficulty in using this book, as there is not much difference between the two editions.

Explanation is called for issuing a key to DDC-19 when DDC-21 has already been published and the work on DDC-22 is already half way through. It has been noted that in India DDC-19 is still being taught in many library schools across the country. But correspondingly there is a dearth of books on this particular edition. It is an endeavour to provide such schools a class text with many illustrated examples for practice of DDC-19. Many examples have been taken from 2000 AD literature.

Suggestions for improvement are requested and will be valued on merit.

M.P. Satija

CONTENTS

1

INTRODUCTION TO THE TEXT OF THREE VOLUMES

The first edition (1876) of the DDC was a thin pamphlet of 44 pages*; and the second edition (1885) was seven times as large as that. This obesity went on increasing. The unwieldy size of the 14th edition (1942) became a source of worry for all concerned. The 15th edition (1951) was an exercise to trim the system to a standard edition, which proved a *faux pas* by every account. To cope with the alarmingly increasing size, the sixteenth edition (1958) was issued in two volumes—the second volume contained the form divisions, areas table and the index. The eighteenth edition (1971) was issued, for the first time, in three volumes, and so is the nineteenth (1979). The first volume contains the introductory material and the various auxiliary tables. The second volume contains the schedule and the third is devoted almost exclusively to the relative index. A companion volume to DDC-19 is the *Manual on the Use of Dewey Decimal Classification Edition 19* (Forest Press, 1982, 551p. ISBN: 0-910608-32-6 It provides guidance in classifying difficult areas. The purpose is to provide a tool for uniformity in interpretation based on the Library of Congress practice

For a skilful operation and better use of the DDC it is expedient to understand the physical structure of the text of three volumes as it stands in the 19th edition.

Volume 1. The first comparatively thinner volume of 482 pages contains the prefatory material by the Publisher (pp. xi-xiii), the Chairman DDCEPC (xv-xvii) and the most important of all "Editor's Introduction"

* A Classification and subject index for cataloguing and arranging the books and pamphlets of a library. Amherst, Mass, 1876, 44 p.

(pp. xxi-lxxv). It also contains a Glossary (pp. lxxvii-lxxxii), a valuable feature of the DDC introduced since the eighteenth edition. The Glossary sufficiently explains all the technical terms used in the Editor's Introduction, as well as implicit in the making of the schedules. The second part of this volume contains the seven auxiliary tables. End material contains a list of relocations and reused numbers given in the classified sequence. This end material is indispensable in reclassifying books with the new edition. This volume ends with three summaries of the DDC schedules. These summaries may help to visualise at a glance the structure and scope of various subjects as laid out in the DDC.

It goes without saying that this Editor's Introduction is very essential to understand the DDC with all its intricacies. However, some librarians especially outside North America feel that its wording is difficult. They demand an easy version. Their demand is not ingenuine. (Meeting this demand this introduction in DDC-20 and DDC-21 has been made much simpler)

Volume 2: The second volume of 1574 pages contains the schedules of class numbers given in numerical order from 001 to 999. In the 17th edition, this was known as the Table. The schedules have been defined as "The series of numbers constituting the notation for the ten main DDC classes and all their subdivisions". This is in fact a full burgeoning of the ten main classes in the hierarchical order. This volume may be called *terra firma* of the book as to learn the practice of the DDC is mostly to learn to operate and interpret this volume. Each entry contains a class number on the left and on its right is given the rubric i.e. the subject meanings. The subordination and coordination relations are shown by the length of the class number on the left and the change of indentation on the right side headings.

Under many of the class numbers are given variety of notes of "explanations and instructions". To locate and build a correct class number, these are very essential. Some of them are explained below:

1. Definition notes

Such notes define the scope and jurisdiction of the class number. For example, the class number 379.11 Financial administration in public education, contains a note: "Costs, expenditure, allocation and management of funds, budgets, budgeting, financial reports". This scope note explicitly connotes the areas which may not be too obvious from the heading given against the class number. Sometimes a simple and formal definition of the subject is given, for example under 020 Library and Information Science, one finds a useful definition of the subject. Some definition notes are explained through examples: under 343.0742 Specific kinds of (economic) assistance, one reads the note: "Example: loans, price supports, subsidies, mortgage insurance". Purpose of both these kinds of notes is the same i.e. to bring to the surface the hidden or extraneous subtopics of a subject, and to demarcate its boundaries as in DDC.

2. Inclusion notes

Some subtopics are not necessarily the part of a given number, but are given a standing room, may be temporarily, with the broader number. For example, 530.41 Solid-state physics contains the note: "Including thin films, electron theory of metals". It means that the topics such as thin films are not essentially a part of the solid state physics and yet these do not have a separate number of their own. Hence such subjects have been given a standing room till they get their own number. *No standard subdivisions are to be added to such class numbers.* However, such notes do not apply to the subdivisions of the topic.

3. "Class here" notes

Under a class number, sometimes there are enumerated some subtopic(s) with the instruction "Class here...". Such topics in fact are broader than the class number, and only for some convenience are to be placed there—usually violating the canon of helpful sequence. For example, under 343.08 Regulation of trade (Law), one reads the instruction: "class here commodity exchanges and exchange transactions". The tenor of such notes is clear.

4. "Class elsewhere" notes

This is in direct contrast to class here notes. When a topic seemingly forming a part of a broader class is granted an independent class number, the broader class number affixes a note in the form: "Class ... in ...". For example, 181.12 Philosophy of Japan contains a note "Class Shinto philosophy in 181.095 61". Similarly, 379.11 Financial administration in public education contains a second note : Class sources of funds in 379.13. Such a note may also be given for related topics having independent class numbers. For example, under 181.4 India (philosophy of), one reads a note "Class Philosophy of Pakistan and Bangladesh in 181.95". Such a note corresponds to "See also" cross reference in an alphabetical index.

5. "Formerly" notes

When in a new edition, as a result of relocation, a subject gets a new number, its previous number is also given at the new place. The former class number is enclosed within square brackets with a prefix *"Formerly"*. For example, 287.5 Methodist Churches in British Isles, also contains a note within square brackets i.e. *[Formerly 287.97]* (Italics theirs). The purpose is to mark the changes between two successive editions.

Related to this type of note are the class numbers enclosed within square brackets, for example, [581.075] Collecting botanical specimens. The class numbers so bracketed are not in vogue and should not be used. Use of some of such class numbers, especially in 920 Biography is optional. In fact, such class numbers have been relocated to a new but more appropriate place. Such bracketed class number always contain a class elsewhere note immediately below it. For example, under [581.075] We find a note : "Do not use; class in 579.6". And under 579.6 we also find a note i.e. [*formerly* 581.075]. And at the new place, a note with *"formerly..."* indicates its previous number, as shown above.

Such a note has a twofold purpose : firstly it clearly delineates the changes between the new edition and the previous one ; secondly it makes clear to those who used the previous edition that there has been no mistake or omission in printing but the number has been surely reallocated.

The vacant sections have also been enclosed in square brackets, indicating in the previous edition when the number was filled with some subject meaning in the schedules.

For example :

[484] Unassigned
Most recently used in Edition 16

It simply means that the section 484 has remained vacant since the 17th edition.

To repeat again, in the 19th edition one additional use of square brackets has been made in 920 Biographies. Now optional numbers have also been enclosed within square brackets. In the previous editions the biographies were collected under 920-928. Now in the 19th edition, the biographies of subject experts have been dispersed by subject, except for generalia biographies which have still been retained at 920. For subject biographies the standard subdivision 092 is to be used. At the same time, the previous arrangement has also been retained for those who may still prefer all biographies to converge at one place under 920-928. All such transferred class numbers have been enclosed within square brackets with the instructions that the use is optional; and the officially preferred treatment has been described under 920.1–928.9 (p. 1445, v.2). For example

Biography of an economist 923.3 or 330.092. Former is an optional number and the later is officially preferred number.

Similarly at [848.99] French language literatures not requiring local emphasis, one finds a note that the use of this number is optional for libraries. Under such notes the official preference, i.e. the class number used by the Decimal Classification Division of the LC is also given. For example, after the instruction under [848.99], the official preference i.e. "Prefer 840-848 for literature of all countries..." has also been indicated.

Similarly, wherever another place for a subject is available, this is indicated with a note "If preferred, class with..." This is an option which is not used by the Decimal Classification Division of the Library of Congress (USA), the official laboratory of the scheme. But if it suits any individual library this option may be availed of. For example, under 016 Subject bibliographies and catalogues one reads "If preferred, class with the specific discipline or subject, using 'Standard subdivisions' notation 016 from Table 1, e.g., Bibliographies of astronomy 520.16". Some critics feel that in such options the value of system as a tool of standardization is eroded.

6. Centered Headings

Sometimes a subject instead of being assigned a single class number is spread over to a span of numbers, the two terminal numbers are connected by a hyphen. These centered headings or entries may occur at the section level or at its subdivisions. These are always given in the centre of the page and on the left margin a pointing triangle indicates a centered heading.

For example:

➤	383-384	Specific kinds of Communications.
➤	384.1-384.7	Telecommunication

It is clearly a breakdown of hierarchy but permits unusual space for expanding the number. Centered heading is a typographical device in the schedule. Therefore, in practice, it is not to be used as such by the classifier. A single class number is always indicated for comprehensive works on the topic. Under ➤ 384.1-384.7 one reads the instruction "Class comprehensive works in 384" Hence single class number for telecommunication is 384. The device of centered headings is very useful for the hospitality and brevity of notation.*

7. Dot and spaces

It is too obvious and familiar to say that all the numerals used in the DDC are decimal fractions. But for the sake of simplicity, the decimal point has not been put in the beginning, it is supposed to be there. But when a number gets lengthened beyond three basic digits a dot is inserted between the third and the fourth digit. This dot is only a pause and must not be misunderstood as the decimal point. It has no purpose except to psychologically break the monotony of numerals.

Again, for the same purpose, if a class number extends beyond six digits a space is left between the sixth and the seventh digit, and again between the ninth and the tenth digit. On this pattern, a space is left after every three digits coming after the dot. For example, the class number for "Bose-Einstein Statistics" is rendered as 530.133 2 and not as 530.1332. Similarly the class number for solid state masers is transcribed as 621.281 336 1. These spaces and dot give relief to the eyes and facilitate shortwhile retention of the class number in the memory—during the passage from the catalogue to the stacks.

8. Number building notes or instructions

Such a note is central to the grammar of the DDC and backbone of the synthetic apparatus in the system. Almost every class number in the DDC can be further extended whether there are instructions or not. For example, the Table 1, of Standard Subdivisions may be added to any class number. In addition to such intrinsic provisions many class numbers are provided "Add..." notes which may further be subdivided into two kinds:

* Comaroni, John P. and Satija, M.P.: *Brevity of Notation in Dewey Decimal Classification,* New Delhi: Metropolitan, 1983, pp. 39-40.

8.1. Individual instructions

Under many a class number are provided instructions for extending a given number with some other full number or part there of a class number existing elsewhere in the schedule. For example, under 547.35 "Quantitative Chemistry" is given the instructions "Add to base number 547.34 the number following 544 in 544.01-544.98". Such cases are usually illustrated with at least one example.

8.2. Instructions common for a series of numbers

Sometimes a series of cognate class numbers are further extendable by another number. Instead of providing individual instructions, for convenience and simplicity, as well as for brevity of the schedules, instructions are provided at one place, while the headings of the class numbers to which such instructions apply are marked with asterisk. Then at the foot of that page a footnote is given reminding the meaning of the asterisk.

For example:

547.4	*	Aliphatic compounds
547.41	*	Hydrocarbons
547.411	*	Paraffins (Alkanes)
547.412	*	Olefins (Alkenes)
547.413	*	Acetylenics (Alkynes)

In the footnote on the same page is given the instruction: "*Add as instructed under 547". On going to class 547 one reads the detailed instructions : "Add to notation for each term identified by * as follows :

04	Special Topics of General applicability
044	Theoretical Chemistry
045	Physical Chemistry
046	Analytical Chemistry
0464	Qualitative
0465	Quantitative"

We can synthesise a large variety of class numbers with such provisions. For example:

Theoretical Chemistry of Hydrocarbons
547.41 + 044 = 547.410 44
Analytical Chemistry of Hydrocarbons
547.41 + 046 = 547.410 46

Such instructions have provided crystal clear citation order of the various facets, hence have increased the number building power.

In addition, there are instructions under many a class number to add from any of the seven tables.

All these instructions must be carefully followed and implemented to build a correct class number. To operate the DDC schedule follow these clearly worded instructions.

Volume 3. It comprises 1217 pages and contains exclusively the relative index. Brief instructions (p. x) and a key to the abbreviations used in the index (pp. xi-xiii) precede the text of the index. Relative index is considered as one of the enduring contributions of Melvil Dewey. It is of great help to the classifiers, and many prefer to approach the schedules through the index. The index is called relative as it brings together all aspects of a single subject which have otherwise been scattered by discipline in the schedule. Hence, the schedule and the index are complementary to one another. Over the years, it has acquired much sophistication, so the relative index has been explained and studied in a separate chapter.

2

BASIC PLAN AND STRUCTURE

The DDC is a general classification System. It aims to classify documents of all kinds falling in any area of knowledge. The entire human knowledge has been divided into three disciplines. These three great divisions are divided into nine main areas of knowledge that are themselves divided into disciplines or sub-disciplines. This division into the nine main classes mirrors the educational consensus of the late nineteenth century Western academic world (and is influenced by the collection of the Amherst College library. The DDC scatters subjects by discipline, and the subjects are subordinated to discipline—any subject may occur in almost any discipline. For example, the subject *metals* may turn up in metaphysics, religion, the social sciences, the natural or physical sciences, technology, and the arts, and may appear several times within the same discipline. Thus there is theoretically no single class number for any subject.

The DDC, true to the times and country of its origin, is a practical scheme. Some would say, and have said, that a consideration of its theoretical grounding, sources, and the order of its main classes is not a profitable exercise.

Before Melvil Dewey there were classification systems based on the subject contents of books, and the decimal notation was employed by many. He had no ambition of improving upon the subject orders that the various existing systems provided. His problem was different (and in this he was practical): he wanted to invent a device which could mechanize shelf arrangement and at the same time provide an appropriate place for the incoming new subjects without disturbing the established order. He did not ponder over much upon the order of the main classes, though the DDC's order mirrors the academic consensus of its time.

Dewey borrowed his basic plan from William Torrey Harris, who had devised the classification for the St. Louis (Missouri) Public School Library. Whatever the case, this matter is no more than of scholastic interest, especially in light of the fact that the scheme now through its various devices and revisional techniques endeavours to reflect the current consensus of scholars in both the order and collocation of subjects.

Dewey's originality lies not in intellectual structure but rather in the notation he used to represent it. Notation has always been underrated by theoreticians and overrated by practitioners and the library's public. Those who write about the making of a classification invariably pronounce that intellectual structure must precede the assignment of notation; this is probably an ideal worth expressing but not holding, for the notation one employs determines intellectual hierarchy and subdivisional capabilities. If one develops a system without bearing in mind the notation to be used, a misshapen classification is bound to result. Dewey fitted his structure to his notation, which is one of the reasons the DDC has been so successful.

He decided to indicate the subject contents by 1-9 notation. Indo-Arabic numerals possessed zero (0), a device capable of providing the notation for a general class, such as 010 Bibliography, and for general aspects of a special subject, such as 510.7 the study and teaching of mathematics; Indo-Arabic numerals were more widely understood as a self-evident order; and Numeral fractions were superior to alphabetical fractions.

It is the last point that gives both power and complexity to the notation Dewey devised. The Dewey Decimal Classification is not so named because a "decimal" point is placed after the third digit of every number having more than three digits. The point is quite meaningless; it is merely a device for promoting visual comprehension of class numbers. The system is decimal because it is a base-ten numerical system. Actually Dewey employed only the fractional part of base-ten numbers; his numbers therefore, are decimal fractions. Now, it is the nature of base-ten numbers that place gives meaning: each number to the left of the point is ten times greater in units than the previous number, each number to the right one-tenth smaller in units than the previous number. In the case of decimal fractions every subunit is a part of the unit to the left. Therefore, by using decimal fractions Dewey not only appropriated the simplest self-evident order but also effected the capability of expressing logical hierarchy, something that integers cannot do.

The ten main classes of the DDC are assigned notation 0 to 9, from

.0000001 to .9999999 so to speak. The notation has a metaphysical side. If we say that 0 is nothing and that 1 is the universe, then the notation (and therefore the substance) of the DDC represents, or is capable of representing, everything in the intellectual universe. The ten main classes ought to be transcribed as follows:

0.0	Generalia
0.1	Philosophy and related disciplines
0.2	Religion
0.3	Social sciences
0.4	Language
0.5	Pure sciences
0.6	Technology (Applied sciences)
0.7	The arts
0.8	Literature (Belles-lettres)
0.9	General geography and history and their auxiliaries.

But in practice, for ready comprehension and simplicity of notation the first zero and the point are not given, but they are understood to always be there. Instead a point is put after the first three digits. This is mathematical nonsense, of course; such a point is never placed between the digits of a decimal fraction. The point is placed here to break up a number so that the mind can grasp its parts more readily. (Experience with telephone numbers tends to support the assumption.) Nevertheless, the point presents a riddle: the point is where it is not, and not where it should be.

Another semantically equally useless and regrettable convention is the minimum of three digits in every class number. If a class number stops short of three digits, the required number of zeroes are used to fill the vacancies. For a main class we have to add two extra zeroes, for a division one. But true to mathematical conventions no decimal fraction may end with a zero after the point; they are redundant and probably misleading (inasmuch as they suggest to novices that the DDC notation is made up of ordinal integers rather than of ordinal decimal fractions).

Notation and Division of Main Classes

The ten main classes are notationally transcribed as:

000	Generalia
100	Philosophy and related disciplines

200	Religion
300	Social sciences
400	Language
500	Pure sciences
600	Technology (Applied sciences)
700	The arts
800	Literature (Billes-lettres)
900	General geography and history and their auxiliaries.

The order of the main classes represents a mix of Baconian and Hegelian philosophy adulterated by the practical needs of organizing a collection of books. Practicality enters the structure of the DDC even at this the earliest of levels: philosophical systems do not require a generalia class, but library classification systems do to account for works that treat all subjects or are applicable to all subjects, such as systems, computer science, bibliography, general organizations. Another example of meeting practical need comes at 800 where one of the arts—literature—has an entire main class to itself, of course, literary warrant demands such notational allotment. As for Baconian philosophy, one can discern in the main classes the three departments of learning made possible by the structure of the mind that Elizabethan thinkers espoused; that is, the mind has three faculties: memory, imagination, and reason—from these are derived the three departments of learning : history, poesy, and philosophy (history, works of the imagination [art], and science). Thus, 100 through 600 involve reason, 700 and 800 art, and 900 history (of places and people). As for Hegelian philosophy, one cannot decry the evidence at first perusal. Study reveals, however, that W.T. Harris, who devised the intellectual structure that Dewey used for his classification, thought that Bacon's structure was a good one, but not for the reason given.

Each of the ten Main Classes has been subdivided further into what are technically known as divisions. Each main class has nine divisions and a general division that is the class itself subdivided into characteristics peculiar to itself or applicable to all of the nine divisions. For example, at 530 one finds the standard subdivisions that represent such things as dictionaries of physics, serials on physics, the terminology of physics, and the like; one also finds mathematical physics, states of matter, instrumentation and dimensional analysis, all topics of general use throughout the subdivisions proper of 530 physics. We have, therefore, 10 main classes and 90 divisions. Here are the divisions of a main class:

600	Technology (Applied sciences)
610	Medical sciences
620	Engineering and allied operations
630	Agriculture and related technologies
640	Home economics and family living
650	Management and auxiliary services
660	Chemical and related technologies
670	Manufactures
680	Manufacture for specific uses
690	Buildings

Each of the 90 divisions has been further divided into nine Sections. For example, 610 Medical sciences, Medicine has been divided as

610	Medical Sciences, Medicine
611	Human anatomy, cytology, tissues
612	Human Physiology
613	General and personal hygiene
614	Public health and related topics
615	Pharmacology and therapeutics
616	Diseases
617	Surgery and related topics
618	Other branches of medicine
619	Experimental medicine

Continuing the decimal pattern, each section can be divided into what we may call Subsections, all being four-digit numbers.

614.1	Forensic medicine (Medical jurisprudence)
.4	Incidence, distribution, control of disease
.5	Incidence, distribution, control of specific diseases
.6	Disposal of dead

It may be noted that 614 is not divided into nine subdivisions. Not all sections require nine subdivisions; it is as simple as that. Problems for the editors crop up when more than nine are needed as is the case for 616 Diseases.

The subsections may be divided into Sub-subsections:

614.51	Salmonella, bacillary, enteric, influenzal diseases
.52	Eruptive diseases (Exanthemas) and rickettsial diseases

.53 Protozoan diseases
.54 Miscellaneous diseases
.55 Parasitic diseases
.56 Zoonoses
.57 Bacterial and viral diseases
.59 Other diseases

Subdivision may continue until literary warrant no longer exists; that is, 614.51 can be divided down to 614.512 Bacillary diseases, and this to 614.5128 Tetanus. There we stop subdividing the topic, though there may be subdivision of the literature on the topic: a dictionary of public health dealing with tetanus 614.512803 (in German 614.51280331).

The DDC has been criticised for its rigidity of division by nine at every step of its division. Division by nine has been likened to the procrustean bed.* The major argument put forth by critics is that knowledge does not proliferate into nine branches at each stage of development. The growth of knowledge is not conditioned by any decimal or metric system. Division by nine is, according to these critics, a rigid and an artificial mould into which knowledge has been structured through force and violence reminiscent of Mr. Procrustes. The criticism is well taken. Here the notation has assumed the role of a master as it dictates its own conveniences. It distorts the structure of knowledge that the DDC tries to represent.

It imparts a regularity and symmetrical pattern to the structure of the classification, thus promoting a powerful mnemonic capability. The decimal notation is simple to understand and apply; it provides infinite hospitality; it shows subordinate and coordinate relations among subjects.

Chain Structure

As noted above, the scheme is hierarchical in nature. It not only collocates the related material but also depicts through its notation the whole-part relations of subjects. It can be argued that the hierarchical pattern that the DDC so finely and easily depicts would stem from the notation he chose. Whatever the case, it is an asset of the DDC which later

* John Comaromi explains the procrustean bed (Eighteen Editions, pp. 633-34): Procrustes was a Greek innkeeper who provided bed and board to travellers, but with a twist from normal practice. According to the legend, he forced his guests to literally fit the bed. If the guests were too short, they were stretched until their feet touched the footboard and their head the headboard. If the guests were too tall, they were simply shortened to the proper length.

classificationists have admitted borrowing from the pioneering system. Progressive specificity is made visible by the lengthening chain of digits. Every progressive step of the unpeeling of a topic is accompanied by the addition of at least one digit to the immediately superior number. For example:

300	Social sciences
330	Economics
332	Financial economics
332.1	Banks and banking
332.11	Central banks
332.110952	Central bank of Japan

The subjects denoted from 300 to 332.110952 build a chain of concepts, as they are in progressive subordination. In the schedules the chain of decimal digits is not depicted typographically, as it is otherwise quite discernible through the increasing length of the class number at each step. These subordination of terms is shown through the change of indentions to the right at every step. Chain analysis provides a mental ladder to arrive at a specific subject as each rung takes us nearer to our area of search by a progressive narrowing. (An added dividend: hierarchical notation is highly susceptible to computerisation.

Hierarchical structure also ensures that the instructions applicable to a given heading are equally applicable to all its subdivisions throughout the chain. (Just as the characteristics of parents are passed on to their children.) This is called the Drip principle. There are exceptions to it, however, these will be discussed at the appropriate place.

Array Structure

An array is a sequence of mutually exclusive entities of equal rank arranged in some chosen order. The main classes, divisions, and sections of the DDC are three different arrays of classes. Array formations can be carried forward to any depth. For example, all the subsections (fourdigited class numbers) of a particular section form their own array. The class numbers 531.1 to 531.9 form the array of 531 Mechanics. Quantitatively speaking, all the equal-digited class numbers, all having the same genus, form an array. Genealogically speaking, all the children of a father form an array, while the family lineage forms a chain. Genealogical charts provide chains and arrays at the same time because they are two-dimensional charts. Classifications, on the shelves cannot provide chain and array structure at a glance.

Pattern in DDC Structure

The position of an entity in an array is not very important provided the array is exhaustive one. Nevertheless, the order of the elements of an array tells us what is most important in the array and reveals the structure of the class the array represents. Over the years increasing synthesis in the DDC has emerged with recognised pattern.

The first subdivision of an array is generally given over to generalia topics, and the last division usually either expounds the historical and geographical treatment of the subject or is reserved for the rest of the unaccommodated topics, which are dumped together as "others". Thus the 9 "others" is a great hospitality device with the scheme.The array of the ten main classes (the first division of the universe of knowledge in the DDC) well illustrates this pattern, as the first division 000 denotes generalia subjects and the last 900 represents geography, history, and other subjects. Pattern at the macro level is repeated at the micro level.

To illustrate the above array pattern from 320, we see that the 320.0 array represents the generalia topics of political science, and the 320.9 represents the historical and geographical treatment of the subject. If we investigate a little more the texture of the arrays, especially the third summary, we will see that the second and third sections of a division are generally made to represent the energy facet, and the rest of the sections in the array represent the personality facets.This can be illustrated from the array of 630 Agriculture. Here 631 and 632 are two sections (dealing with the problems of agriculture) that can be added to the other sections and their subdivisions, i.e., 633-635, which represent the personality facet i.e. produce of 630 Agriculture. The above pattern can be seen in 540 Chemistry and 580 Botany; it can be seen elsewhere and almost everywhere. Such a pattern in the texture of the DDC is not widespread due to its early foundations, but is something that the structure of the DDC tends to reflect in the face of the increasing synthesis and the restructuring of the classes where possible.

Hospitality

Hospitality of a classification is defined as its ability to accommodate the emerging topics at their proper places without dislocating the already existing ones. The longevity of a classification system is directly proportional to the efficiency of the hospitality devices employed.

Hierarchical notation provides infinite hospitality upon the given base and deterred somewhat by other practical realities: theoretically there is no limit to the further elongation of a class number to any point demanded by the co-extensiveness of the subject. A newly-emerged independent topic hitherto forming an indistinguishable part of an already existing one may be easily accommodated at the end of the chain by adding another digit to the class number of the parent topic. It is an easy as to stretch an elastic cord. Hierarchy also makes it possible to adapt the DDC in any library, whether small, medium, or large.

One disadvantage of the purity of notation inherent in the DDC's decimal fractions is that the accommodation of a new subject in an array is not easily done. If a new, independent subject emerges in-between and coordinate with a class, say 510 Mathematics and 520 Astronomy, it is impossible to allot an appropriate place for such a subject. To avoid such a situation, one course of action is to leave some gaps in the notation that describes an array. For example, in the array 511-519 of mathematics, 517 and 518 have been left unassigned. If ever a new branch of mathematics is developed, space is available (if the branch falls logically between geometry and probabilities).

In the third summary (the third level of subdivision in the DDC) there remain 86 unused classes; these are shown in the schedules by having their three-digit figures enclosed in square brackets. For example [136] [unassigned] Some of these gaps may be used in the future. And gaps exist in all the arrays onward at any level—the more remote the array the greater the possibility of a home for a subject. The leaving of gaps is not a science; it is an art for its day. And the day may come when all the gaps are gone, but new subjects will continue to emerge—and spin as we cannot turn our back upon them. Gaps are few in main class 600 Applied sciences, where subjects still emerge dynamically. Moreover, the chain there has already been elongated to the limit of tolerance.

Another way to account for emerging fields is to redo several contiguous divisions, as has been done for 350-354 Public administration, 560-590 Life sciences in DDC-21 (1996).

The DDC is not the same as it was when created a century and quarter ago. It has undergone constant changes; opened itself to latest developments in classification theory and information science and information technology. During its existence it has shown its mettle in the arena of bibliographic classification theory. What has remained stable is its basic plan, its notation, and its desire to serve librarianship.

3

HOW TO ASSIGN CLASS NUMBERS IN THE DDC

Work of practical classification consists of two distinct phases: intellectual work in sorting out the specific subject of the document under classification; and the craft of assigning the appropriate notations to the ascertained specific subject—yes, it is a craft, a mechanical work. These two phases can be likened to medical diagnosis and prescription respectively. If the ailment is correctly diagnosed then prescription for its cure can safely be administered by junior physicians. Former is an intellectual work, and for that reason the most important of the two. It is indeed the essence of classifying and somewhat independent of the classification system used. Determination of the specific subject of a given document is something of an elusive art. It is no exaggeration to say that it requires a tinge of intuitive insight. It easily comes through wide acquaintance with knowledge. This knowledge may constantly improve all through one's life, though may never reach perfection. Indeed, widely read people have more flair than others in determining the specific subject of a book. Indeed, a classifier has to be a jack of all.... Intense specialization and very rapidly advancing frontiers of knowledge have, nevertheless, made it more difficult rather nearly impossible to know something about every subject. It is something which could be expected of scholars with encyclopaedic knowledge such as Aristotle, Pythagoras, Francis Bacon, Leonardo da Vinci, Benjamin Franklin, Herbert Spencer, and lastly Bertrand Russell and Lala Hardyal who considered all knowledge as their province. It is atrocious to expect this much from lowly lying classifiers, a class of academicians with very humble knowledge and moderate intellect. It is not to suggest that to be able to assign an appropriate class number from a classification schedule one needs the intellect of Bacon or Russell. Far from that, an average librarian learns to do this job satisfactorily well.

Subject Analysis

The specific subject of a document may be determined by examining the document under classification through its title, sub-title, preface, blurb, table of contents, and the text itself. The name(s) of the author(s) subject index and the cited references may also provide some valuable clues. A classifier may occasionally consult some reference tools for help in this task. If all these efforts fail one to arrive at the specific subject, the last resort is to consult some subject expert. This so far is the work in the domain of knowledge classification. Besides determining the specific subject of a book, there may arise many difficulties to class especially a composite book at its appropriate place. For all such difficulties one can surely count on the classic book W.S. Merrill: *Code for classifiers: Principles governing the consistent placing of books in a system of classification.* Chicago: A.L.A., 1969, 189p. This book is independent of any classification system.

A librarian is always concerned with book classification, as distinguished from the work of knowledge classification. Therefore, for book classification, besides the knowledge of *knowledge qua knowledge,* one needs to know the structure of knowledge, its subdivisions and various adjuncts in a particular system of classification. It is the work of match making: fitting in the subject into an already created pigeon-hole. A classifier is essentially a match maker. To do this is needed the schedule and the technique to consult it. Contrary to Ranganathan's views the work of a classifier is more a matter of flair than anything else. Once the specific subject is determined decisively, the further need is to determine the core subject and its way of treatment by the author in context of the classification system used : that is, determine from what viewpoint the subject has been treated. For example, a subject, say Economics, may be treated from the viewpoint of its philosophy, theory, history, research or from practical applications viewpoint. Further the above document treated from any above mentioned viewpoint could be a dictionary, a journal or a mere collection of data in tabulated form. Not only this, any of the above internal or external arrangement may reach us in any of the numerous physical media, namely a book, microfiche, video cassette, a film or a phonorecord, a CD-ROM or a multimedia item. Thus a classifier has to sort out three different aspects of a given document. After this is done, the only task left is to codify the subject and its treatment view-point into the decimal notation. First we codify the core subject then its viewpoints and physical media into decimal language and integrate these notations.

To enter the Decimal Classification, the better way is through its structured ladder (The other way is through the index, which will be discussed in the chapter on 'Relative Index'). One must know at the outset (through knowledge of the scheme) to what main class, and then to what division and finally to what section of the DDC the given work pertains. For efficiency, it is better to commit to memory the 100 Divisions of the scheme. It is not absolutely necessary, though it surely lessens the avoidable leafing the page of the DDC schedules to assign a class number. With experience, many of the thousand sections come on one's fingertips. In this way, we go on narrowing our search successively at each step. Many a time we straightway reach the section concerned through our personal knowledge of the scheme bypassing the scanning of ten main classes and its 100 divisions. If a subject is concerned with say education, we will go to 370 part of the schedules; and if it is concerned with medicine we look at 610 in the schedules. Even if one is not conversant with the 100 Divisions, this much part of the class number should be worked through the three summaries given on pages 471 to 482 (Volume 1) of the DDC. The real need to consult the schedule arises on arriving, at the correct sections. To carry on the search for appropriate and specific class number all the immediate divisions of a section, viz, subsections are further scanned, which for the convenience of the classifiers are usually given at one place. For example, all the subsections of 515 Mathematical Analysis are given in multilevel or window type summary on page 626. These multilevel summaries have a great reference value, and save the time and patience of the classifier in nabbing the desired class number. In this way the search is carried down to the last level desired.

A classifier is like a traveller who has to select his path at every crossing where many roads diverge in various directions. By choosing the right direction at every step the classifier does not have to scour after the whole text to reach the desired class number (classifier will get lost if at any crossing a wrong path is followed). In this way the minutest number available may be the specific number desired or that may only act as the base number to build further the coextensive class number matching exactly with the subject of the document under classification. The further extension of the class number may be either from the auxiliary tables or schedules. (This is discussed in the concerned chapters).

To illustrate this, say our subject is "Money". At the first instance we need to determine the discipline, by examining whether the core subject of the book is minting of money or economics of money. If latter is the case, a knowledgeable DDC practitioner will tell at the outset that it is a subject of social sciences, then economics. On going to 330 Economics in the third summary (Volume 1, p. 476) we see that it pertains to 332 Financial economics. At this stage, we shift to the schedules proper at class number 332 (Volume 2,.p. 261) Examining the summary of subsections of 332 (Volume 2, p. 263) we find the subsection 332.4 Money, matching squarely with the subject of the given document. By assigning, the class number 332.4 to the document our search for the appropriate and specific class number ends.

Take one more example, "Anatomy of Human lungs". The book deals with a human body organ, so in a twinkling, a practised classifier can tell that it belongs to the main class Applied sciences, and then to its Division medicine, which deals with human body machine, its parts and functions. Looking through the Division 610 Medicine, we find that Anatomy (which is the science of Human organs) is 611, which is the desired section. At this stage we shift our search to the schedules at 611 (Volume 2, p. 828). Looking through the summary of the subsections of 611 (on page 829) we find that 611.2 Respiratory system is the next appropriate choice. Examining the further divisions (subsections) of 611.2 (page 830) we find the "Lungs" enumerated at 611.24, which is our specific number. If the subject is "Study and teaching of lungs anatomy", the Dewey classifier will know that "Study and teaching" is an auxiliary aspect of the core subject "Lungs anatomy", and the notation for the auxiliary aspect is to be taken from the Table 1: Standard Subdivisions. Both the notations are to be combined as per rules.

In fact this is too facile a view of the process of assigning a class number to a document. In reality, a classifier may encounter many unheard and unimagined difficulties. Firstly, it may be borne in mind that we assign class numbers not to the title but to the specific subject of the document under classification. If the title is a fanciful one and the subject not explained in the subtitle (which usually is done) the specific subject of the book may be determined from the other places in the book. For example, a book with the title "Asian Drama" is not a book of creative literature but on the economic developments in the Third World. Sometimes the title may look incomplete, For example, a book may have a title "Shakespeare". At the outset one may not know whether it is the biography of Shakespeare, or his evaluation as dramatist, or poet, or merely a collection of his works. To classify correctly one will have to supply the wanting words from other parts of the text. On the other hand there may be many superfluous words in a title, which is usually the case. In such cases the title must be stripped of such meaningless but decorative words, and the class number be assigned only to the core words connoting the subject succinctly. For example, a book may have the title "A Long and Exciting Expedition to the Himalayas". Here Himalayan expedition is the core subject and for the purpose of classifying one will have to ignore the remaining words, however, spiritually or emotionally important for the author. Melvil Dewey's "Introduction" to the 12th edition of the DDC (1927) is also of still great use in this context. S.R. Ranganathan's eight step for classifying a document may be of great help to a novice classifier.*

Above all the difficulty may ensue from the fact that no word in the title may be redundant, yet it may not be possible to assign a co-extensive class number to whole of the title. Take the title "Classification in School Libraries". In the DDC the class number for classification is 025.43 and that for school libraries is 027.8. There is no provision to integrate these two numbers. Here we will have to make a choice. Editors usually advise us to choose the more concrete of the two, which usually comes later in the schedules. Many a time, the Order of Precedence may be given: as under 362 Social welfare problems and services; and again at 362.79 Problems of and services to other classes of young people; and also at 363.1 and 364. Table of precedence is also given for the Standard sub-division in Table 1. Choice may also depend upon author's emphasis, or needs of the individual libraries.

Similarly, a book may treat more than one subject at a time. The classifier will have to choose a generic class number if possible or give class number for one of the subjects and ignore others. The reason is that the DDC still aims to group documents broadly as contrasted from the faceteers ambition to make classification an artificial language of notation translating equivalently the subject of the book into the notation used. DDC does not aim to provide a unique class number for every document in the library. In reality it is an impossible task for any classification system.

Yet another difficulty may lie for the new subjects yet unenumerated in the schedules. In such cases the book may be assigned to the closest possible broader class number, which may cover the subject of the book. In such cases, the standard sub-divisions are not added to the class

---

* S.R. Ranganathan: *Colon Classification.* 6th ed. Bombay: Asia, 1969. pp. 1.7-1.8 [Later reprinted by the Sarada Ranganathan Endowment, Bangalore.

number, even if the subject specially demands this. It is done with the hope that the new edition may probably provide a specific class number. In such a case the coextensive class number may be provided by just adding a digit or two to the previous number, and the number from auxiliary tables may be added then. For example, a book may be "A Dictionary of Reclassification in Libraries". Here, we will have to put the book under classification 025.42, as there is no separate number for reclassification and the standard subdivision for dictionary is not to be added. For such problems the editors have provided guidance in DDC-19 Volume 1, Sec 8.711-8.72 (pp lii-liv).

Another but more important problem may be of interpreting the schedules as per intended meaning. In spite of so many scope notes, and cross references, it is still an elusive task. However, some difficulty has been lessened by the publication of the *Manual on the Use of the Dewey Decimal Classification: Edition 19* prepared by Dr. John P. Comaromi and his team (Forest Press, 1982). It provides interpretations of the class numbers and the headings used as done by the Decimal Classification Division of the Library of Congress where the schedules are mostly prepared and first used. It is hoped by the Forest Press that this work will bring about more efficient, effective and more standardized use of the DDC. Even then subjectivity in interpretation cannot be ruled out; and the subject analysts may disagree among themselves on the connotations of a heading and on the question of assigning a correct class number to a given book. J.B. Friis-Hansen aptly says that "Identical use of DC in all countries is impossible and hardly any chance of it exists. Identical classification of the same book is a difficulty, in one country, even by one person on different week-days"* CIP data MARC Record, various national and trade bibliographies** using the DDC, *Manual on the Use of the DDC-19* help to lessen this inevitable problem to a good extent.

---

* J.B. Friis-Hansen "What Dewey Knew" *Libri 26* (3), Sept, 1976:223.

** Namely American Book Publishing Record (ABPR) and the British National Bibliography (BNB), Indian National Bibliography (INB).

4

NUMBER BUILDING PRACTICAL

Synthesis through "Add to...." instructions from the schedules.

(a) Add to from 001 to 999
(b) Add to from some slice of a class number from some other small portion of the schedules.
(c) Add to from the same division/section.
(d) Add to through special provision (facet indicator) including the 04 general special:

Most of the specific subjects have readymade class numbers in the schedules as the DDC is basically an enumerative scheme. While for some other especially multifaceted subjects the number will have to be built on a given base number. The choice of the base number is the most important step to build the desired number. Ranganathan's facet formula is of much help in such matters, but that is no substitute to the familiarity with the DDC schedules. Every base number contains sufficient instructions in clear words to subdivide that number by any other class number or part thereof

On arriving at a specific number, it may be seen too frequently that if still required the number may be further sub-divided by some number or its part as taken from the schedules itself. Broadly the above kind of additions may be divided into four categories (a) to (d) as above. One general advice is that the decimal number should only be put after the first three digits when the whole number has been built.

Addition of any number from the whole schedule viz, 001-999.

It seems easiest, as to the designated base number, one is required to add another whole number from the schedules. It is as easy as that.

025.46 is library classification of specific disciplines and subjects. For library classification of any discipline one finds the instruction that to the base number 025.46 add 001-999. It means, we are to add the class number of that subject to the class number 025.46, e.g., Classification of books on mathematical analysis:

025.46 + 515 = 025.465 15

(515 is the class number of Mathematical analysis)

Similarly, "Library Classification of Indian Philosophy" will get the class number

025.46 + 181.4 = 025.461 814

(181.4 is Indian philosophy)

Similarly 026 libraries devoted to various specific disciplines is to be further subdivided like 001-999 for the class number of any library devoted to any specific subject

Science Libraries

026 + 500 = 026.5

Terminal zeroes being redundant in a decimal figure have been removed in the ultimate class number

Libraries of library and Information Science

026 + 020 = 026.02

Libraries devoted to Indian Philosophy

026 + 181.4 = 026.181 4

Library on Inorganic Chemistry

026 + 546 = 025.546

069.9 Museum devoted to specific discipline and subject are subdivided like 001-999 as per instruction for a museum devoted to specific subjects.

Museums of Zoology

069.9 + 590 = 069.959

Museums on Space flight

069.9 + 629.41 = 069.962 941

Science Journalism

070.449 + 500 = 070.449 5

331.124 Job Vacancies and opportunities (Labour Economics)

331.1241 Job opportunities in occupations other than extractive, manufacturing and construction industries.

For job opportunities in Military Service: to the designated base 331.1241, as per instructions, we are to add the class number of Military Science taken from the schedule.

331.1241 + 355 = 331.124 135 5

Job opportunities in Library and Information Science

331.1241 + 020 = 331.124 102

Job opportunities in Public Libraries

331.1241 + 027.4 = 331.12410274

Student Societies and Organizations

371.83

Student Organizations in specific fields

371.84

It is to be further subdivided by 001-999 for student societies on specific subjects. To the base number 371.84, we are to add the class number of that subject.

Students Chemical Societies

371.84 + 540 = 371.845 4

Society of Library Science students.

371.84 + 020 = 371.840 2

Literary Societies formed by students

371.84 + 800 = 371.848

Educational Curriculum

375

As per instructions under 375.01 – .09, curriculum for any specific subject is to be got by adding to the base number 375, any appropriate number falling between 010-990*

Curriculum in Library Science

375 + 020 = 375.02

Curriculum in Dewey Decimal Classification

375 + 025.431 = 375.025 431

---

* Here it may be noted that the range has been narrowed down to 010-999 from 001-999. Therefore, any number falling outside this range will not be admissible. For example, Curriculum in Cybernetics 375.001 53 is not an admissible class number.

Take another example:

778.53 Motion Pictures photography

778.538 Photography of specific subjects

To this base number, we are required to add the class number of the subject concerned for its Cinematography.

Motion-picture Photography of Birds

778.538 + 598 = 778.538 598

Many more such examples can be enlisted of topics admitting further division by the whole range of the schedules. However, this device is not to be used of its own: Classifier can use this number building device only on invitation, though one may be tempted to use such methods at one's own initiative.

* One thing quite obvious is that whenever a class number admits further division from 001-999, ss (Standard subdivision), if required, for that subject is added with three zeroes, as two zeroes may be used sometimes for a subject class number. In such cases instructions exist for addition of a standard subdivision with the required number of zeroes.

Curriculum in Library Science

375.02

Directory of Curricula

375.000 25

Here directory is a standard subdivision.

Similarly,

History of libraries devoted to various specific disciplines

026.000 9

General libraries—A periodical

027.005

Add to some designated base a portion of the class number from some smaller area of the schedule

Instead of admitting a whole class number from anywhere in schedules a designated base may require addition from some specific part of the schedule, from a single main class or division or a section or even smaller than that. It is only a specialised extension of instructions "Add to ...." from 001-999. In such a case instead of adding the whole class number to the specified base number a portion of a smaller number is added. Here the initial common digits from series of class numbers are removed, and

* Read this paragraph on Second reading of this book.

the digits following these digits are added. This makes the resulting class number brief, without any ambiguity. There can be no difficulty in retranslation of the class number into ordinary language, too. For example,

181 Oriental Philosophy

181.04-.09 Oriental Philosophy based on specific religions.

To derive the class number for any specified religious philosophy, we are instructed under 181.04-.09 to add the number following 29 in 294-299 to the base number 181.0. For example,

Buddhistic philosophy

The number for Buddh religion is

294.3

Here the digits after 29 are "43". These are to be added to 181.0. The derived number thus is:

181.0 + 43 = 181.043

Similarly

Confucious Philosophy

Confucianism is a religion, with the class number:

299.512

Hence the Confucious philosophy will get the class number

181.0 + 9512 = 181.095 12

Let us take another example:

331.2	Wages...of Labour
331.204	In specific industries
331.2042 — .2049	In extractive, manufacturing, construction industry.

For a class number for wages/condition of working in any specified industries related to manufacturing, extractive or construction, we are required to add to the base number 331.204 the number following 6 in 620-690

Wages of Agricultural Labour

The number for Agriculture is 630 and the digits which follow 6 are 30. So 30 is to be added to the base number 331.204.

Hence

331.204 + 30 = 331.204 3—

Working conditions in Mines

331.204 + 22 = 331.204 22

(The class number for mining being 622)

395 Etiquettes

395.1 Etiquette for specific ages and sexes.

The class number for Etiquette of a spcified sex or age groups is to be got by dividing 395.1 (Base number) like 170.2022 – 170.2024

It means we are to add to the base 395.1, the number following

170.202 in 170.2022 – 170.2024

Etiquette for Men

395.1 + 232 = 395.123 2

Etiquette for Children

395.1 + 22 = 395.122

Whereas the class number for Ethics of Men and Ethics of Children are

170.202 232 and 170.202 22 respectively.

Take another example:

578 Microscopy in Biology

578.4 Use of Microscopes

For the use of specific types of Microscopes, we are to extend 578.4 like the subdivisions 535.332, which enumerates the kinds of microscopes:

535.332	Microscopes
535.3322	Simple Microscopes
535.3323	Compound Microscopes
535.3324	Ultramicroscopes
535.3325	Electron Microscopes

Therefore, the corresponding numbers of Microscopes in Biology are:

578.4 + 2 = 578.42	Use of Simple Microscopes (in Biology)
578.4 + 3 = 578.43	Use of Compound Microscopes
578.4 + 4 = 578.44	Use of Ultramicroscopes
578.4 + 5 = 578.45	Use of Electron Microscopes

Some more examples:

Wheat trade

380.141 + 311 (from 633.11 wheat) = 380.141 311

Air conditioning in Secondary School Buildings

697.93 + 72 (from 727.2) = 697.937 2

Air conditioning in law school buildings
697.93 + 743 4 = 697.937 434
Reviews of documents in Microforms
028.13 +6 (from 011.36)
= 028.136
Reviews of Braille books
028.16 + 3 (from 011.63)
= 028.163

"Add to.... " From the Same Division

There is a subtle difference between "add to. . ." instruction from the same Division/Section, and the number being added from some remote part of the schedules. This difference lies not in the method, but in the nature of the part of the number added. As said earlier, a Division is so further subdivided into sections, that second and sometimes (third also) section enumerate the action facet, while rest of the section enumerate the personality facet to speak in the Ranganathan language. These personality facets from section XX3 - XX9* are further divisible by the facets of XX1 or XX2; thereby giving the general citation order as personality followed by action. Exceptions are however there to this citation order. Therefore, actually it is an addition of a secondary facet. One can say without reservations that this technique has made the scheme really multifaceted. There seems not much difficulty in adding such a facet. It is more easy in light of the fact that one has not to flip many pages of the schedules, Frequently occurring characteristic of such a facet is that, this "add to..." instruction occurs not alone but one finds instructions to add a part of a particular numbers to a series of topics. Therefore, instead of repeating instructions at every class number, the editors give instructions at one place, and the class numbers or base number in this context susceptible to such a facet are marked with an asterisk *. The meaning of asterisk is explained at the footnote of every page where asterisked base numbers occur. Another characteristic is that such a facet is generally added through a facet indicator, prescribed under the instructions. For example, take the title

COTTON HARVESTING

Here cotton is the concrete subject, so will form the base number.

---

* The first X denotes the Main class and the second a Division.

Obviously this is a subject of agriculture; going to 630 Agriculture we find the number for Cotton at

633.51 * Cotton (Gossypium)

It is marked with an asterisk, which at the page footnote explains: "add as instructed under 633-635". Going back to the instructions given at page 1041, we find a series of instructions. The very first instruction is relevant to our purpose. We are asked to add to the base class number, the digits following 631.5 in 631.51—631.57. The class number, for Harvesting is 631.55. It means that as per instructions, we are to add to 633.51 the number following 631.5 i.e. 5 only. Therefore, the complete class number for Cotton Harvesting is

633.51 + 5 = 633.515

Similarly, we can add to 633.51 the whole series of number from 631.51—.57

Soil preparation for, Cotton

633.51 + 1 = 633.511

Cotton Seeds

633.51 + 21 = 633.512 1

New varieties of Cotton

633.51 + 23 = 633.512 3

Cotton Yield

633.51 + 58 = 633.515 8

Cotton Storing

633.51 + 68 = 633.516 8

Take another example:

Reproduction in Protozoa

In this case protozoa with class number 593.1 will form the base number. Here we are told to add as instructed under 592–599 (p. 795). Instruction relevant to our purpose is 04 General Special, it means for general principles i.e. (action facet) we are to add first 04 to the designated base and further add the number following 591 in 591.1—591.8

In 591 the number for reproduction is 591.16. Therefore we are to add only "16" to the above compound number

593.1 + 04 + 16 = 593.104 16

Here "04" only acts as a facet indicator. The general principle that emerges out is that we can add all the subdivisions of 591 to all the class numbers from 592–599, though a facet indicator either 0 or 04.

Reproduction in invertebrates

Class number for Invertebrates is

592

General principle of Invertebrates

592.01 — .08

For a specific general principle, we are asked to add to 592.0 (Zero being, a facet indicator) the number following 591 in 591.1–591.8.

Class numbers for "reproduction" is

591.16

Thus we are required to add 16 to 592.0. The complete class number therefore for Invertebrates Reproduction is :

592.0 + 16 = 592.016

Similarly, we can build a series of class numbers on the base 592.0 for general principle of Invertebrates.

Physiology of Invertebrates

592.0 + 1 = 592.01

Biophysics and Biochemistry of Invertebrates.

592.0 + 19 (from 591.19) = 592.019

Evolution of Invertebrates

552.0 + 38 (from 591.38) = 592.038

Anatomy of Invertebrates

592.0 + 4 (from 591.4) = 592.04

Ecology of Invertebrates

592.0 + 5 (from 591.5) = 592.05

and so on.

*It may be noted that since 0 has been utilised as a subject facet indicator, so all the standard subdivisions from Table 1 should be added with a double zero:

Dictionary of Invertebrates

592.003

Journal of Invertebrates

592.005

Experimental Research in Invertebrates

592.007 24

But wherever the General Principle facet is added through "04" the standard subdivision can be added with the normal zero:

---

* Read this paragraph on second reading of the book.

Dictionary of Protozoa

593.103

Study and teachings of Protozoan Zoology

593.107

Take another example:

Chemical Kinetics of Alkaloids

Basic number for Alkaloids is

547.72

Here, we are asked to add, as per the footnote, as instructed under 547 (on page 697). Since Chemical Kinetics is a topic of Physical Chemistry, so, the third instruction i.e. 045 Physical Chemistry is relevant to us. Here, we are asked to add to 045 the number following 541.3 in 541.34 – 541.39.

It means 045 is a compounded facet indicator.

Number for Chemical Kinetics is

541.394

The digits following 541.3 are "94" in this case. Thus the complete class number for the title in question is

547.72 + 045 + 94 = 547.720 459 4

In this manner we can extend any class number in 546 and 547. For Example

Optical properties of Alkaloid solutions

547.72 + 045 + 414 = 547.720 454 14

Thermodynamics of Chemistry of Alkaloids

547.72 + 045 + 69 = 547.720 456 9

Facet indicator for adding from the subdivisions of 541.2 is 044 as per the same instructions.

Stereochemistry of Alkaloids,

547.72 + 044 + 23 (from 541.223) = 547.720 442 3

Quantum Chemistry of Alkaloids

547.72 + 044 + 8 = 547.720 448

Similarly in 294.4 Jainism, General Principles of Jainism have been placed in 294.41–.48. These General Principles can be further individualised as in 291; for this we are asked to add to the base 294.4 the number following 291 in 291.1– 291.8. Let us take an example.

Sacred books of Jains

Our base number is 291.4 and the number for sacred books in 291 is 291.82. Thus to the base 294.4, we will add "82". Hence the class number for "the sacred books of Jains" is

294.4+82=294.482

Similarly,

Jain Eschatology

294.4 + 23 (from 291.23) = 294.423

Sacred places for Jains

294.4 + 35 = 294.435

Worship in Jains

294.4 + 43 = 294.443

Jain Saints

294.4 + 61 = 294.461

Some of the most important examples of such a synthesis occur, however, in 350 Public Administration where 351 is Central Governments (theoretical principles). All the Central Governments of various countries except US Government, have been put at 354.3–.9. For Central Government of a country, we are asked to add to the base number 354, the area notation for that country from the Table 2. For example:

Union (Central) Government of India

354 + 54 (T2) = 354.54

Central Government of Italy

354 + 45 = 354.45

For specific organ or aspects of the executive of the Central Government, we are required to add to the resulting class number, a zero and further add the digits following 351.00 in

351.001 – 351.004. For example:

President of the Government of India

For Government of India we have

354.54

and as per instruction (page 444) to this base we will add a zero = 354.54 + 0 and further we will add to it the digits following 351.00 in 351.00313, viz. "313". Hence the complete class number for the India's President is

354.54 + 0 + 313 = 354.540 313

Similarly,

Queen of Great Britain

354 + 41 (Area Table) + 0 + 312 (from 351.00312)
= 354.410 312

Vice-President of India
354.54 + 0 + 318 = 354.540 318

Cabinet of Jammu & Kashmir Government
354 + 546 (T2) + 0 + 4 (from 351.004) = 354.546 04

Similarly,

Indian Ministry of Finance
354.54 + 06 (as under 354.3–.9, p. 444) + 2 (as under 06)
= 354.540 62

Indian Ministry of Defence
354.54 + 06 + 6 = 354.540 66

Some more examples:

Powers of the US President
353.03 + 22 (from 351.00322) = 353.032 2

Powers of the President of the Republic of India
354 + 54 (Area Table) + 0 + 313 (from 350.00313)
= 354.540 313

This is in fact the class number for the President of India, as the further extension is not possible.

Term of Office of the Prime Minister of India
(the Chief Executive)
354 + 54 + 0 + 34 (from 351.0034) = 354.540 34

Cabinet of Madhya Pradesh
354 + 543 (Table 2) + 0 + 4 (from 351.004)
= 354.543 04

Ministry of Finance, Government of Punjab
354 + 545 52 (Area Table) + 06 + 2 (From 351.02)
= 354.545 520 62

Problems in Acquisition of Government Publications
025.28 + 34 (from 025.173 4) = 025.283 4

Book Selection in National Libraries
025.218 + 75 (from 027.5) = 025.218 75
(Area can also be added to 027.5)

Book Selection in the Library of Congress
025.218 + 75 + 73 (Table 2) = 025.218 757 3

Reference Service in Children Libraries

025.527 + 7625 (from 027.625) = 025.527 762 5

Cataloguing and indexing of Microforms
025.34 + 94 (From 025.1794) = 025.349 4

"Add to ...." From the Same Section

Sometimes some special facets, applicable to all the subdivisions of a Section are enumerated in the beginning of the same section. These special facets are of general applicability within the same section. Instructions are provided against each subsection and their further divisions to add the desired facet. Take for example, the title:

Heart Diseases Physicians
or Heart Specialists or Cardiologists

For heart diseases, we will have to go to the section dealing with all the diseases in medicine 610. The number for diseases is 616; and the specific number for heart diseases is

616.12 (Diseases) * of heart

Here an asterisk leads us to the footnote which instructs us to add as instructed under 616.1– 616.9. Going to this bulk of instructions on (pp. 868–869), we find the number for Physician is 0232 and it is directly attachable to the base number:

616.12 + 0232 = 616.120 232

Similarly,

Prevention of Heart Diseases
616.12 + 05 = 616.120 5

Case studies in Heart Diseases
616.12 + 09 = 616.120 9

In such cases, since the subject divisions have usurped the original place of the standard subdivisions, therefore, the standard subdivisions are advanced to the place beginning with a double zero:

Research in Heart Diseases

616.12+0072=616.120 072

Similar instructions are also found under the subdivisions of 618

618.1 Gynaecology

618.11 Diseases of ovary

As per similar instructions one can add to this number any required facet enumerated under the heading 618.1–618.8

Preventive measures for ovary diseases

618.11 + 052 = 618.110 52

Surgical treatment of ovary diseases

618.11 + 07 = 618.110 7

Take another example

746 Textile arts and handicrafts.

To many of the subdivisions of 746 may be added special subdivision given under 746; and whenever these special facets are admissible such places have been marked with an asterisk.*

Crochet Patterns:

Under 746 the specific class number for crochet is

746.434

and as per instruction we add to it the number for "Pattern" given on pages 1283.

Thus the complete class number is:

746.434 + 041 = 746.434 041

Pattern in Woven Carpets

746.72 + 041 = 746.720 41

Similarly, under 787–789, "other" instructions and their music, many special facets have been enumerated, which can be added as explained before, to the subdivisions in 787–789

Guitar programmes

781.61 + 0739 = 781.610 739

One can add area notation from Table 2 to 0739, if required:

Guitar Programmes in U. S. A.

781.610739 + 73 (T2) = 781.610 739 73

Guitar Scores

781.61 + 5 = 781.615

Take another example in 546 Inorganic chemistry. Here almost all the individual elements are extendable by some special facet enumerated once for all in the beginning under the general heading 546 Inorganic chemistry. The instruction here is: Add to each subdivision identified by* as follows:

1	The Element
2	Compounds
22	Acids and bases
24	Salts
25	Complex compound
....	
5	Physical chemistry
6	Analytical chemistry
....	

For example, if the subject is

Potassium salt

Class number for Potassium is

546.383

and "Salt" is a Special facet having number "24".

The complete class number for Potassium salts, therefore is:

546.383 + 24 = 546.383 24

Similarly, the Special facet for "Physical Chemistry" of individual elements is "5". As per instruction, it is further divisible as the subdivisions of 541.3 as in 541.34–541.39. We are to add to 5 the digits following 541.3 in 541.34–541.39

Take for example

Physical Chemistry of Potassium

546.383 + 5 = 546.383 5

Chemical Kinetics of Potassium

(It is a topic of Physical Chemistry)

The base number is

546.383

Since it is a Physical Chemistry aspect, so we add 5

546.383 + 5 = 546.383 5

The digit "5" is further extendable by the subdivisions of 541.3

The class number for Chemical Kinetics is

541.394

The digits that follow 541.3 are "94". Hence the complete class number for Chemical Kinetics of Potassium is

546.383 + 5 + 94 = 546.383 594

Similarly,

Isotopes of Potassiun

546.383 + 5 + 88 = 546.383 588

Photochemistry of Potassium

546.383 + 5 + 5 = 546.383 55

Quantitative Analysis of Sodium

546.382 + 65 = 546.382 65

Some of the facets applicable to some of the subdivisions of 721–729 specific aspects of architecture have been enumerated thereunder on page 1238

722 Ancient and Oriental Architecture

722.11 Chinese

It, as per instruction, admits a facet enumerated under 721–729

Maintenance and repair of the Chinese Architecture

722.11 + 0289 = 722.110 289

Preservation Theatre Buildings

725 + 82 + 0288 = 725.820 288

Architecture of Buildings for physically handicaps

725.54

(Here there is no need of adding "42" from the facets given under 721–729)

Preservation of Knitted laces

746.22 + 0488 = 746.220 448

Repair of Woven rugs

746.72 + 0489 = 746.720 489

Scores of Children Songs

784.624 + 06 = 784.624 06

Collection of Duet Songs sung by Children

784.82 + 1 (from 784.306 11) = 784.821

5

ORDER OF PRECEDENCE

Notwithstanding so many synthetic devices, sometimes we may not be able to provide a co-extensive class number for a given micro subject having many facets. Theoretically, such facets could be combined but the DC schedule does not allow them to combine together in a single class number. (It is puzzling as to why the schedules do not allow the combination of facets especially when such situations are identified, and the feasibility and literary justification of their combination is also admitted). Inevitably in such cases some facets will have to be ignored. The problem arises which facet is to be chosen, and which facet is to be ignored. As a general rule, more specific facets are preferred over the less specific facets. But this weighing of specificity is not left to the arbitration of the classifiers. Many a time sufficient guidance is provided. Under many a generic class numbers or central heading, the schedule provides a Precedence Table, which determines the priorities of the two or more class numbers, giving clear direction as to which class number is to be chosen in case of choice between two or more class numbers. The table of precedence for the Table 1 (of ss) has been discussed in the chapter on Standard Sub-divisions:

In the schedules, for example, under 155.42–155.52 Psychology of specific groupings, the schedule gives the following Table of Precedence:

Exceptional Children	155.45
By class, type, relationship.	155.44
By age groups	155.42
By sex	155.43

For example, take the subject "pre-school girls." Here girls, and pre-school children are different subdivision of 155.4 and the schedules do not provide any instructions to combine them. The different possible class numbers are:

153.423	Pre school children
153.433	Girls

As per the table of precedence given above, 155.42 and its subdivisions are to be perferred over 155.43 Sex psychology. Hence the correct class number for Pre-school Girls is 155.423 and not 155.433. Similarly,

Psychology of Exceptional girls

155.45

Psychology of Gifted boys

155.45 + 5 (from 371.91 – 371.97 where gifted children is 371.95) = 155.455

Here as per precedence table, we ignored the facet boys, and further elucidated the preferred number as per instructions under 155.45.

Table of precedence occurs at 351.84 Social Welfare and corrections

Another table of precedence is given at 362 Social Welfare Problems and Services.

Providing Welfare Service to Poor Women

Services to alleviate Poverty is 362.5

Services to Women is 362.83

As per Table of precedence under 362 (page 469, Vol. 2). 362.83 is to be given precedence over 362.5. Hence the correct class number is 362.83

As per this table

Administration of service to handicapped poor

351.844, not 351.845

Adminstration of service to mentally ill young people

351.844, not 351.848

Similarly,

Welfare Services to the politically oppressed veterans

362.87 and not 362.86

Problems of poor South Asians (South Asians are a national group)

362.84 + 914 (Table 5) = 362.84914 and not 362.5

South Asian's Family problems and relief services.

362.82 and not 362.84914

Another precedence table one finds at 641.5 Cookery

Vegetarian cookery for travel

641.563 3 and not 641.575

Time saving cookery for armed forces

641.57 and not 641.555

Cooking Breakfasts for South Asians

641.57 and not 641.592 + 914 (Table 5)

Cooking Lunch in School

641.571 and not 641.53

Another table of precedence is given under 649.1

Rearing Pre-School girls

649.123 and not 649.133

Rearing Exceptional girls

649.15 and not 649.133

Rearing deaf boys

649.15+12 (dividing like 371.91–371.97)

= 649.151 2 and not 649.132

Another table of precedence occurs at 657.1–657.9 Elements of accounting (page 1110)

Auditing fixed assets

657.73 and not 657.45

Public accounting for non-profit organisations.

657.98 and not 657.61

Cost accounting in Co-operative Hotels and Restaurants

657.837 + 0 + 42 (Dividing like 657.1–657.7 as per instruction under 657.837) = 657.837 042 and not 657.97

Book Keeping in Non-profiting Hospitals

657.8322 + 0 + 2 (Dividing like 657.1–657.7)

= 657.832 202 and not 657.98

Another table of precedence occurs at 658.304 Management of Specific kinds of personnels (p. 1120):

Management of highly talented Scientific Personnels

658.3094 and not 658.3045

Table of precedence is also given for various

Chemical Compounds based on specific elements other than

Carbon 661.82 – 661.89

Chemical technology of Organometallic Esters

661.895 and not 661.83

Chemical technology of Halogenated Esters

661.84 and not 661.891

Silicon Acids-Chemical technology

661.88 and not 661.86

Aromatic silicon Esters-Chemical technology

661.88 + 6 (Dividing like 661.814–661.816 as per instruction under 661.82 – 661.89) = 661.866 and not 661.83 + 6

Large scale manufacture of Aliphatic phosphoric acids

661.87 + 4 = 661.874 and not 661.86 or 661.864

We find yet another table of precedence at 746.1 – 746.9

Products and Processes of Textiles and handicrafts.

Crocheting tapestries

746.3 and not 746.434

Dyeing rugs

746.7 and not 746.13

Precedence table also occurs at 747.9 Various specific interior decorations :

Interior Decorative lighting for Weddings

747.92 and not 747.93

Interior decoration with houseplants for parties

747.98 and not 747.93

At 757 Painting of human figures and their parts, precedence table is also given :

Paintings of Nude Women

757.4 and not 757.22

Miniature portraits of Men

757.7 and not 757.3

Precedence Table under 784–789 Individual mediums of musical expression determines the precedence of one medium over another, if a title combines two or more media:

Harp and Organ

787.5 and not 786.6

Choruses and part songs on Violin

784.1 and not 787.1

Usually the schedules occasionally provide guidelines assigning a simple number to a complex subject but at a few other times we have to rely on some general principle and occasionally on our judgement.

When there is no instruction then more specific class number is given precedence over less specific number. One mechanical formula to weigh the specificity of the two class number is : of the two class numbers one with a Zero and the other having no Zero the latter is more specific, hence given precedence. Similarly a class number having one zero is given preferred over a class number having two or more zeroes. It is known as the *Rule of Zeroes.* For example,

Official Status of Gold Coins

332.4222 and not 332.42042

Political Offences by Mafia

364.13 and not 364.106

Administration of Personal Guidance Programmes

371.46 and not 371.4042

Wooden Chairs and Tables

684.13 and not 684.104

Maintenance and Repair of Beds

684.15 and not 684.1044

On the same principle, a class number with one Zero will have precedence over a class number with two Zeroes and so on. For example,

Policy making in Finance Departments of Central Government.

351.02 and not 351.0072

However, one exception to this rule occurs at 262.3—262.4 specific form of church organization:

Government of Roman Catholic Church

262.0 + 2 = 262.02 and not 282

Sometimes the DDC replaces a table of precedence by a single instruction to choose the earlier or later notation. For example at 331.3 – 331.6 Labour force by presonal characteristics we get the instruction:

"Unless other instructions are given, class complex subjects with aspects in two or more subdivisions of this schedule in the number coming first in the schedule....."

For example

Labour by old Women

331.4 and not –3 = 331.52

Labour force of immigrant children

331.31

Sometimes the Table of Precedence is simply replaced by Class Elsewhere Notes. For example, under 025 Library operations one reads the instruction: "Class Comprehensive Works on operations in specific kinds of institutions in 026 – 027". According to this instruction, we have for

Administration of School Libraries

027.8 and not 025.1

Classification in Government Libraries

027.5 and not 025.42

But this formula does not apply to 025.2 Acquisition and Collection development :

Book Selection in specific types of libraries

025.218

Here one reads the instructions "Add to base number 025.218 the number following 02 in 026 – 027"

For example

Book Selection in School Libraries

025.218 + 78 = 025.218 78 and not 027.8

Book selection in Government Libraries

025.218 + 75 = 025.218 75 and not 027.5

Sometimes there may be no fixation of priorities for a given subject, but the general citation order in that class may provide the priorities to be given. For example:

Tillage for Pasture and its grasses

633.202 and not 631.51

as the citation order for 630 agriculture is "Crop-operation":

Similarly

Storing of China Jute

633.56 and not 631.568

In spite of such instructions, the classifiers may have to rely many a time on their own judgement.

The objective of the Order of Precedence Table, Citation Order and a host of notes especially Class reference notes, here or elsewhere is to avoid cross classification and to strike maximum uniformity and consensus in the application and interpretation of the system.

6

USE OF TABLE 1: Standard Subdivisions

Knowledge, which is the predominant basis of library classification, is an abstract entity. It cannot have any form by itself. It requires some physical media for its encapsulation, dissemination, and preservation above all. A document, which is a source of knowledge, has always some physical form. Library classification on the face deals with documents. Library Classification in effect deals with knowledge as contained in documents. Therefore, library classification has to take into full account the outer attributes of these physical objects embodying knowledge. The library classification may be described by the following equation:

Library Classification = Knowledge Classification + Viewpoint of the presentation of the text + Physical attributes of the document = Subject + Internal form + External form.

These documentary forms are both internal and external. For example, it may be expedient in a library to separate a microfilm, or a phonorecord or a disk from a usual book, though the specific subject of these media may precisely be the same. It is equally expedient to distinguish between a dictionary and a periodical of a subject as well as the philosophical viewpoint from the historical one of the same subject.

To account for such physical attributes of the documents, Melvil Dewey in the second edition (1885) separated such non-subject forms of the documents and listed them in the beginning of each Division. These tables could be attached to any class number and always remained the same in name and notation. The notation for such recurring, concepts always starts with a zero and they have meaning only when attached to some class—they cannot be used independently. 'These are described as form divisions, as mostly they stood for the form of the document. In the seventeenth edition (1965) these form divisions were veritably renamed as "standard subdivisions", as these recurring non-subject divisions gathered there had obviously outgrown the form divisions. Now, they include some recurring viewpoints, and even facet indicators as they stand in the nineteenth edition. They are called "standard" because their meaning and notation remain the same wherever they are used. What started truly as "form divisions" have evolved *parri passu* with complexities and varieties of incoming documents, to a conglomerate of some complex but recurring concepts termed as standard subdivisions. The standard subdivisions as they stand in DDC-19 (Volume 1, pp. 2-13) may broadly be categorised as under:

01, Parts of 02, 07 and 09	View points
02 partially, 03, 05 and 06	Internal forms of treatment of subjects
04, 08 and to some extent 09	Facet indicators to introduce a new facet.

Scope of the standard subdivisions has so much been widened that it is advisable to go through the Table 1 (in volume 1) to know their scope and variety. Some standard subdivisions give the illusion of a subject division. A knowledge of their nature and scope will surely add to the efficiency of the classifiers, Rules for adding standard subdivisions to a class number have been provided in Sections 5.24, 8.53 and 8.7 of the "Editor's Introduction" in Volume 1. Here rules have been explained to use Table 1, and some advice is given for the situations where the classifiers may feel intrigued. Some brief instructions to apply them and the Order of Preference also precede the actual Table 1 (page 1, Volume 1) Rules for adding a ss are summarised as follows:

1. Standard Subdivisions are added to the ultimate class number of the document in question. Having reached the most specific class number, we do not necessarily need any invitation to add any standard subdivision.
   Encyclopaedia of Islam
   297 + 03 = 297.03

   (Here Islam is the subject and Encyclopaedia the standard subdivision)
   History of Ahmadiyya Movement
   297.86 + 09 = 297.860 9

(Here we have added ss 03 and 09 respectively, though there are no instructions to do so at these class numbers).

2. Subject whose specific class numbers yet do not exist in the schedules, should not be expanded with any ss. For example,

   Standards for goat's milk

   Here "standards" is a ss whose number is–0218 in (Table 1). Goat's milk is a subject of animal husbandry. Where milk production is 631.1 (which is cow's milk). All other milks are put under 637.17 with no further subdivision. Thus no specific class number has been provided for goat's milk. Therefore, as per rules, we cannot add the standard subdivision here; the correct class number, therefore, is 637.17 and not 637.170218. This is done not because of any structural difficulty; it is an advice to ease expansion in the future. May, be some future edition, depending upon its literary warrant, provides a number for goat's milk, which probability would be a subdivision of 637.17. If the ss is added to 637.17 it may entail total effacing and rewriting when we provide co-extensive class number in conformity with some future edition.

3. Usually two standard subdivisions are not applied in succession to a class number. If a subject poses two standard subdivisions, then only one is to be applied, on preferential basis, and the other is to be ignored. Table of preference is prefixed to the Table 1. If we examine, the preferential order, it becomes obvious that facet indicator general special is followed by viewpoints, and the real form divisions come in the end. It means *internal forms are to be preferred over the external forms.*

Let us take the example "Encyclopaedia of Organisations on "Applied Psychology". Here "Encyclopaedia" and "Organization" both are ss with notation 03 and 06 respectively. Therefore, only one of them is to be added. As per preferential table, "06" is to be given preference over "03". Therefore, the correct class number is 158.06 and not 158.03 or any number combining the two ss viz. 158.0306

Similarly. "Directory of library Schools in India" will get the class number

020.711 54 instead of 020.2554

Therefore, whenever there are two standard subdivisions, this table must be consulted to know which of them is to be applied, and which is to be ignored.

If, however, a class number is susceptible to two standard subdivisions, such cases in the schedule have been spelled out. For example, "Philosophy and theory of Nursing": 610.7301. The class number is enumerated. Here 073 Nursing and 01 Philosophy both are standard subdivisions. Such cases admitting two ss though a few are clearly indicated. However, any standard subdivision from 01-09 may be added to the ss 04. The reasons are obvious: 04 is not a ss in the real sense.

IRREGULARITIES

Extension in Meaning.

If any of the ss when applied to a class get some local name in that context, then in that schedule all such proper standard subdivisions are to be used. In all such cases, the notation is compatible with the Table 1, but the nomenclature is somewhat modified. Striking example of such an extended meaning exists in 610 Medicine. In Table 1, we have – 073 students, learners, apprentices, novices; when it is added to 610 to make 610.73, it gets the meaning "Nursing and other activities auxiliary to Medical profession". Similarly the ss 013 value in context of 331 labour economics has been the meaning: "Freedom, dignity and value of labour".

Also the extended meaning, of ss 01 philosophy and theory exists in the Main Class 700 Fine Arts:

701	Philosophy and theory of Fine and Decorative Arts.
701.1	Appreciative Arts
701.17	Aesthetics
701.18	Criticism and appreciation

Such an extension of the ss 01 does not exist elsewhere. Similarly, the ss 08 Anthologies has been given the extended meaning Rhetoric and collections of literature (irrespective of language) which has further been subdivided as per need.

808	Rhetoric and collections
808.02	Authorship and editorial techniques
808.025	Writing for publication

However, the classifiers should abstain from giving their homemade extended meanings to standard subdivisions, howsoever, demanding the situation be: and howsoever, apt the self extended meaning may appear to them.

Irregular Places

Going beyond the extended meaning some standard subdivisions are shown as subject divisions and consequently moved to a division in the array. It happens in case that compound subject has a subject value and considerable literary warrant. Such a treatment allows further extension of such subjects. This happens usually for the geographical and historical treatment of a subject:

331.2	Wages (Labour economics)
331.29	Historical and geographical treatment of wages, instead of 331.209

To avoid cross classification cross reference is provided from the probable class number likely to be looked by the classifier to the actual number used in the schedules. For example, in the above case, the not used class numbers [331.209] is enclosed in square brackets, and a cross reference here directs the classifier to 331.29. Similarly, techniques, apparatus, material for art metal work is 739.1 instead of 739.028. Though techniques, apparatus etc., is ss but here it has been enumerated like a subject. Similarly, 534.9 is Table reviews, exercises in sound physics, instead of 534.076. Again in 535 optics 535.9 is Reviews and exercises in optics instead of 535.076.

Similarly, 720.9 is Historical and geographical treatment of Architecture. But the architectures of specific ages, instead of being provided in 720.901–.905 have been shifted to 722-724. Accordingly at [720.901–.905] one reads the instructions "Do not use, class in 722 – 724." Therefore:

Medieval Architecture

722 instead of 720.902

Twentieth Century Architecture

724.91 instead of 720.904

Similarly, Historical and geographical treatment of art metal work in gold.

739.227 instead of 739.2209

Consequently:

Goldsmithy around and before 1000 BC

739.227 013 instead of 739.2209013

Another interesting aberration occurs at 666.3 Pottery—Ceramic technology. Here, we are asked to add ss at 666.31–39, instead of at the usual place viz. 666.301–309. Here a Journal of Pottery will get the class number 666.35, and Teaching and study of Pottery will be 666.37 and so on. Not only this, there is one exception to this exception viz. "techniques, procedures, apparatus, equipment, material" another ss, is to be placed at 666.4, instead of placing at the usual 666.328.

Similarly, some other irregularities also occur in case of the use of Chronological Table. In usual cases any chronological period division is to be taken from the Table 1, where the "ss" "09" has been further subdivided as 0901-0905 enumerating all periods of history. These are obviously attachable to any class number, but for some classes, for example 800 Literature, and 900 History, some special "Period Tables" have been provided. Therefore, in such cases these tables are to be used, instead of the general one viz. at ss 09. In fact, in case of Main classes 800 and 900 period is a subject facet, instead of being merely an auxiliary. For example:

20th Century English Poetry
821.91 instead of 821.0904
Elizabethan English Drama
822.3 instead of 822.09032
History of India in 1970's
954.05instead of 954.09047 or even 954.047
England under Elizabeth I
942.055 instead of 942.09031 or 942.031
History of 18th Century Germany
943.05 instead of 943.09033

One more interesting irregularity occurs in 340. The usual place for ss here is given as 340.02.09. For example,

Dictionary of Law
340.03
Study and teaching of law
340.07

But the philosophy and theory of law has been placed at 340.1 with its own extended meaning:

340.112	Law and ethics (Ethics for lawyers falls in 170 ethics)
340.115	Law and society.

Extending the irregular use of the standard subdivisions a bit further, we find numerous cases, where a geographical facet is made inherent in the structure of the class number. In such cases, the geographical facet is not added through the ss 09. For instance

General Statistics of Europe
314 instead of 310.094
General Statistics of France
314.4 instead of 310.0944
General Statistics of India
315.4 instead of 310.0954

Many a time, a classifier finds two places for the historical and geographical treatment of the subject. Both of them have their own meaning. We must learn to perceive through the subtle difference between the subject as an academic discipline, and the actual practical conditions in that field. A good example has been provided by 320 Political Science where

320.09	Historical and Geographical treatment of political science.
and 320.9	Political situations and conditions.

The correct class number for Political conditions in India will be 320.954

Similarly

591.09	Historical and geographical treatment of Zoology.
but 591.9	Geographical treatment of animals (Fauna)

Animals of India and Pakistan
591.954 instead of 591.0954

Similarly,

592	Invertebrate Zoology
592.009	Historical and geographical treatment of the study of invertebrates.
592.09	Geographical treatment of invertebrate Zoology.

592.0954 Invertebrates (found in India)
020.9 History of Library Science
027.01–.09 Geographical treatment of libraries.
History of Libraries in India
027.054 instead of 020.0954

In case of 027, General Libraries, an unusual separation of historical and geographical treatment has been made:

027.009 Historical treatment of libraries.
027.009 045 Libraries of the World in 1960's
but 027.054 045 Libraries in India in 1960's

Similarly, a standard subdivision may be redundant, if the form or viewpoint is already inherent in the subject itself:

Dictionary of English Language
423 instead of 420.3 or 423.03
History of India
954 instead of 954.009
(Which may mean history of historiography of India (not in India necessarily)

Similarly, under 340 Law, use of ss 026 law is redundant, though the use of the latter is itself optional in the 19th edition:

Banking and Insurance Law
346.08 instead of 346.08026

Such examples may be multiplied enormously. It will be an interesting and useful exercise to isolate all such cases of irregular use of standard subdivisions.

Enigma of Zeroes

In Table 1 every ss begins with a featured zero, which is essentially a facet indicator marking the transition from subject divisions to the form division in the class number. The original rules for adding, standard subdivisions, though quite simple and uniform in the beginning, have become rather complex in the face of the warping structure of the DDC. Sometimes a featured zero may seem missing, while at others ss may begin with one, two or even three zeroes. These exceptions to the rule of one zero in ss, so outnumber the normal cases that abnormality is the rule now; and the pristine rules are applicable in exceptional cases. This has happened due to many structural variations in the schedules to accommodate the new subjects. These oddities have been abruptly grafted rather than evolved through. Therefore, some subjects have been prepositioned to usurp the hereditary place of standard subdivisions. For example, 344.05 is not a journal of social law 344, but is subject division connoting "Police services, public safety, public morals and customs". Similarly, 616.07 is not study and teaching of diseases but means medical microbiology. Similarly, 535.014 is Ultraviolet light; instead of terminology of optical physics. Sometimes a subject division may begin with two zeroes, as 351.002 means Finance Department of a Central Government, and 351.004 means Cabinets and councils of State. Since the position for standard subdivisions have been occupied by subject divisions, therefore, in such cases, the standard subdivisions are so designated as to distinguish them from subject divisions to avoid confusion. This is done by denoting the ss with two zeroes or three zeroes as the case may be. Hence, there is no fixed formula for attaching or identifying a ss. The only formula is to follow the instructions, if any, provided in the schedules under a class number. In all such abnormal cases, the adequate and clear instructions are invariably provided. Such irregularities have discounted a great deal the mnemonic value of the scheme, and consequently the efficiency too has been at stake.

Dictionary of Human Diseases
616.003
Philosophy and theory of Constitutional Law
342.001
Journal of Constitutional Law
342.005

In case of 350 Public Administration, ss are to be added with three zeroes, as the subject division start both with one zero or two zeroes.

Study and Teaching of the Subject of Central Government
351.00 7
Journal of Central Government
351.000 5
Journal of Local Government
352.000 5
Journal of US Government
353.000 5

Rules for Adding Standard Subdivisions

Subject to the above rules, a standard subdivision may be added to any class number. If the ultimate class number is a main class or a division i.e. ends with two zeroes or one zero, the zeroes filling the vacant space are to be removed before adding a standard subdivision; and the digits are reshuffled that the dot is put after the first three digits. For example, take a title "Encyclopaedia of Science". Science is 500, and Encyclopaedia is a ss with notation 03. Since in 500 there are two formal zeroes, therefore, these are to be removed.

The synthesised class number is

500 + 03 = 503

Similarly

Journal of Philosophy

100 + 05 = 105

In 510, Mathematics, we have only one redundant zero, so, it is to be removed while adding any standard subdivision:

History of Mathematics

510 + 09 = 510.9

Philosophy of Mathematics

510 + 01 = 510.1

The reader may be reminded here that zero/zeroes removed are those not belonging to the ss but to the class number. The featured zero of the ss is always there.

But these statutory zeroes are not to be removed, or removed partially as the occasion may demand, if the subject divisions have been moved to the places of ss. For example

Dictionary of Social Sciences

300.3 and not 303

Here only one zero has been removed, though there are two redundant zeroes in 300 social sciences. This has been done because the class number 303 has already been assigned the meaning of "Social processes", in Sociology. Similarly, 532.005 is Journal of Fluid mechanics instead of 532.05. which means Dynamics here. Here (under 532) instructions have been provided to use ss at 532.001–532.009. Such instructions do not have a hierarchic force, i.e., ss to the subdivisions of 532 are to be added with normal zeroes, as there will be no ambiguity on that account.

Journal of Dynamics

532.0505 instead of 532.05005

Research in Statistics

532.02072 instead of 532.020072

Here are given some more examples to illustrate the variety and scope of standard subdivisions:

Tools for Descriptive Cataloguing

025.320 28

Library and Information Science as a profession

020.23

Acronyms in Library and Information Science

020.148

Indian History through Pictures

954.002 22

History of Mughal India through Pictures

954.025 022 2

A VCR on the DDC

025.431 020 8

A VCR on the History of the DDC

025.431 09

History of the DDC upto the end of 19th Century

025.431 090 34

Exercises in the DDC

025.431 076

* Many of the Standard Subdivisions may be further extended by synthesis either through Table 2 to 7 or from the schedules.

Optical Principles of Coordinate and Post-coordinate indexing

025.484 + 015 (T1) + 35 (from the class number 535 Optics) = 025.484 015 35

Here 015 Scientific Principle is a standard subdivision which is to be further divided like 510–590 and Optics is 535.

Indian Library Association

020.622 + 54 (Table 2) = 020.622 54

Class Number for a National Library Organization is 020.622 to which area notation from Table 2 is to be added as per instructions.

Universities imparting Library Science education in Maharashtra State.

020.711 + 54792 = 020.711 547 92

---

* Please read this paragraph on second reading of this book.

Under 07 Study & Research –0711 is a ss standing for College and Universities which is further divisible by area.

Research in Library Classification in Canada

025.42 + 072 + 0 + 71 = 025.420 720 71

Life of Melvil Dewey by Wayne A Wiegand

020.924

Autobiography of S R Ranganathan edited by PN Kaula

020.924

Dictionary of Philosophy

100 + 03 = 103

Dictionary of Philosophy in French

103.41

Here 03 has been extended by Table 6 where number for French language is 41

History of Philosophy in India

100 + 09 + 54 = 109.54

(It is not the history of Indian Philosophy). Here the ss 09 has been extended by the Area Table.

Reader Advisory Services to Doctors

025.54 + 088 + 61= 025.540 886 1

Here, the subject has been treated among Doctors (non-racial, non-ethnic, regardless of national groups of people). Here ss 088 has been extended by Table 7, where number for Doctor is 61

Reading interests of Doctors

028.9 + 088 + 61 = 028.908 861

but

Reading Interests of Children

028.55

Here the use of ss 088 and its extension by Table 7 for children will be redundant, as the Class Number itself means children.

Reading Habits of Indians (National Group)

028.9 + 089 + 91411 = 028.908 991 411

is a ss for treatment of the subject among national groups, which is to be further extended by the Table 5, where number for Indians is 9141 1. The use of ss 088 and 089 should be distinguished from -024 which means a work for specific type of users.

Dewey Decimal Classification for Indian Practitioners

= 025.4310240391411

Science for School Children
502.405 44
Child Psychology for Parents
155.402 404 31
Mathematical Statistics for Librarians
– 519.502 409 2
Arithmetic for Managers
5l3.024 658
Political Conditions of the world in the Century
320.905
Politicil conditions of India in the Century
= 320.95405

7

USE OF TABLE 2 : Areas

Whenever a subject is studied within the context of a given geographical area, the ultimate class number from the schedule may be qualified by the area number taken from the Table 2. Need to add area notation usually occurs in Social Sciences and Humanities where the treatment and practice of a subject varies from place to place. Here area is more or less an intrinsic part of the subject. Some other disciplines may also need the area facet occasionally. Where a schedule does not authorise us to add from the area table, the area table can still be added through the ss 09 from Table 1.

This is largest of all the auxiliary tables (pp. 14 to 386 out of the total of 452 pages). Its length consists not in any variety of subdivisions as it is in detail. A brief paragraph of instructions (p. 14) precedes the enumeration of area numbers. All areas of the World, natural geographical divisions, or political or administrative units, or some scattered geophysical divisions of earth or some non-continuous conceptual divisions based on various characteristics of people who habitat them, have been accommodated in divisions 1 to 9. The area 1 stands for the scattered regions bound by some geophysical characteristic or by some social characteristic, e.g. Plane regions, forests, deserts, oceans, socio-economic regions and so on. The digit 2 has been allotted to persons regardless of area, region places. Digit 3 denotes the ancient world; and the modern world as divided into various continents, countries, provinces, cities has been denoted by the notation 4 to 9. Obviously the list for the geographical subdivisions of area number for USA 73 are far more detailed than that of any other country. Here subdivisions have been enumerated upto county level, whereas for many other countries there are no divisions further to states/provinces.

OCEANS AND

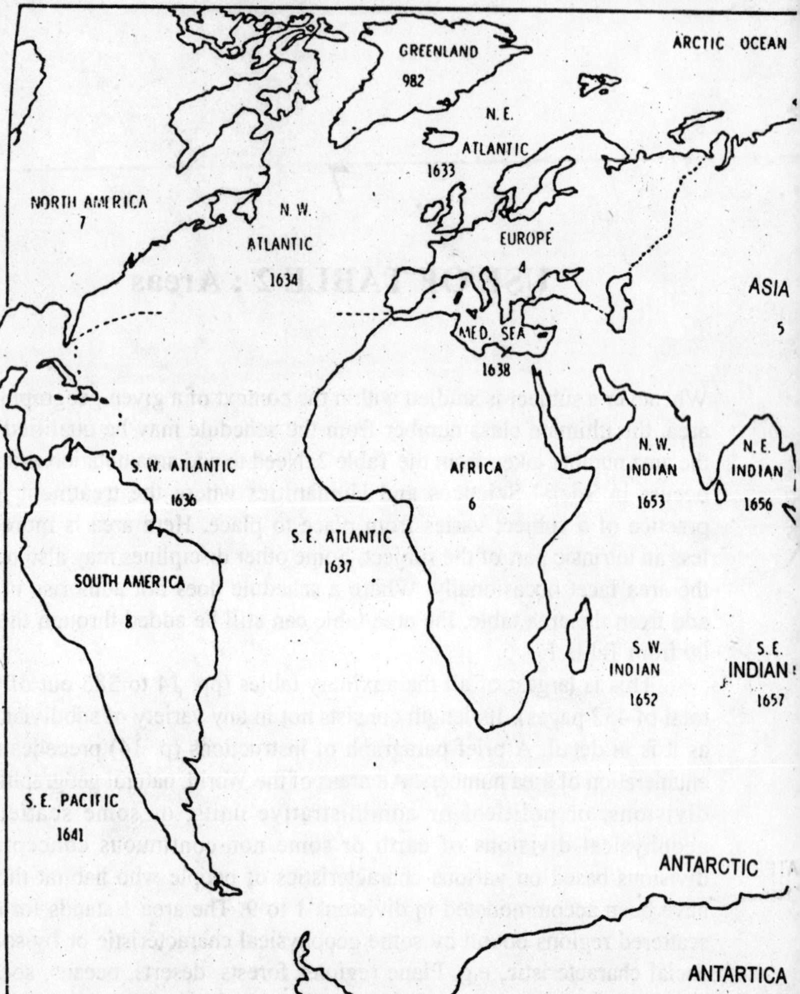

Not to Scale

REGIONAL CONCEPTS

163	ATLANTIC OCEAN	1636	WEST ATLANTIC	164	PACIFIC OCEAN
1631	NORTH ATLANTIC	1637	EAST ATLANTIC	1642	EAST PACIFIC
1635	SOUTH ATLANTIC			1644	NORTH PACIFIC

CONTINENTS

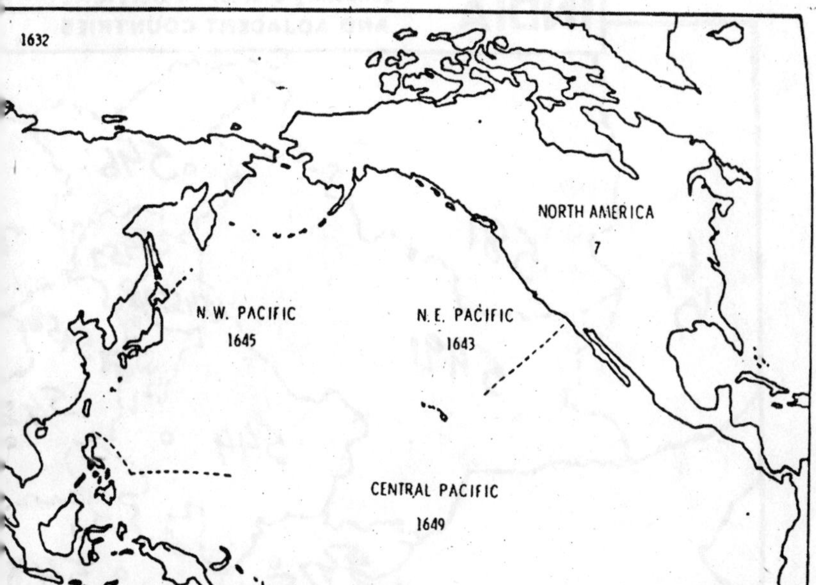

Courtesy: Forest Press, USA

1646 WEST PACIFIC
1648 SOUTH PACIFIC
165 INDIAN OCEAN
1652 WEST INDIAN
1657 EAST INDIAN

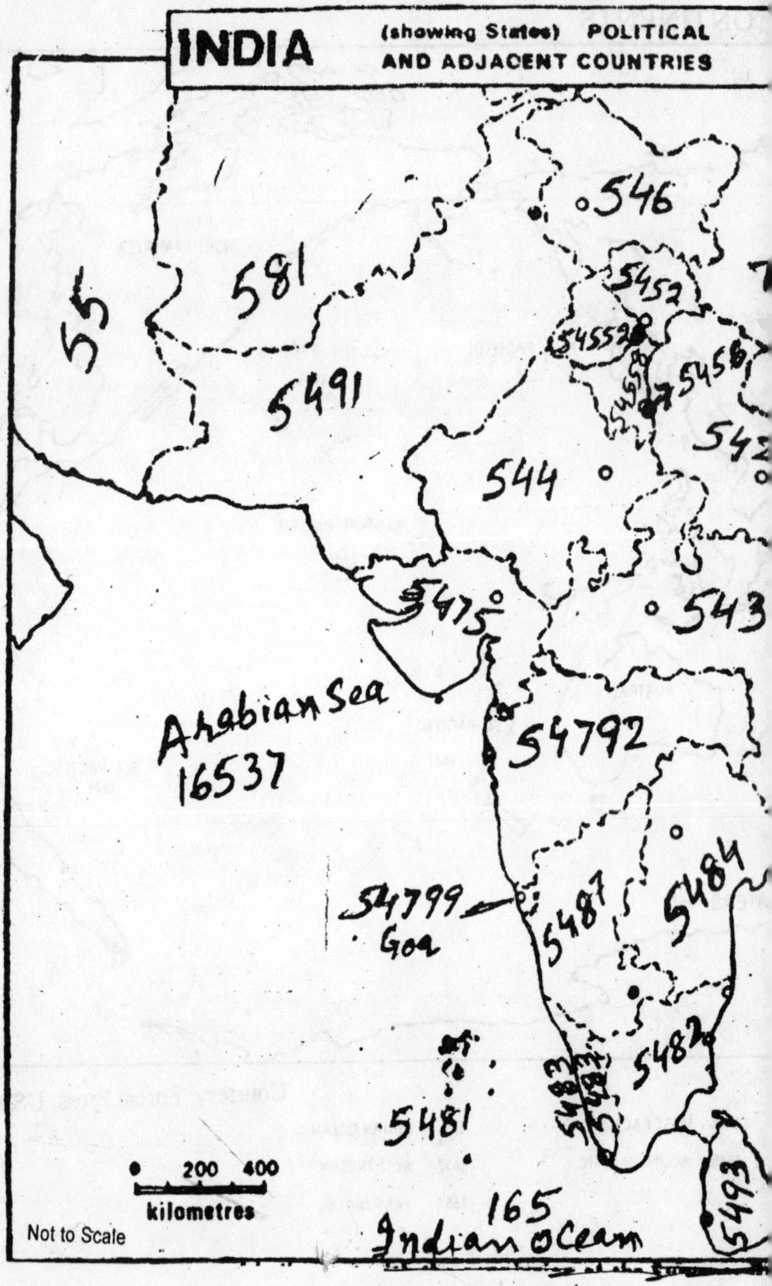
INDIA
(showing States) POLITICAL
AND ADJACENT COUNTRIES
546
5452
581
55
5491
544
543
5475
Arabian Sea
16537
54792
54799
Goa
5487
5484
5482
5481
5483
5493
200 400
kilometres
Not to Scale
165
Indian Ocean

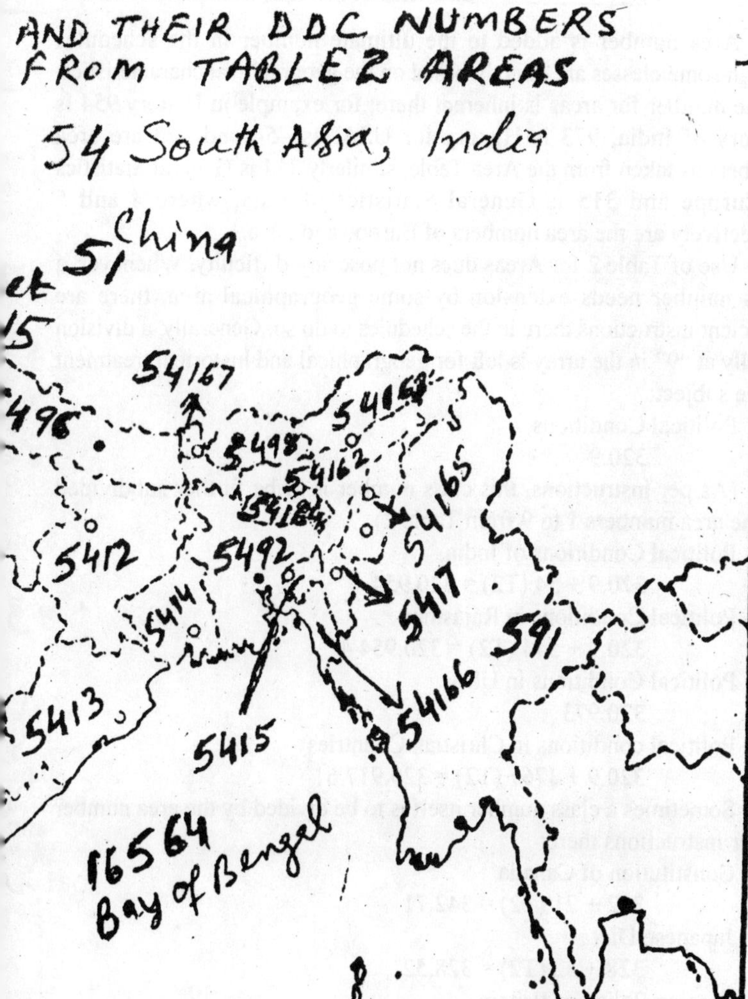
AND THEIR DDC NUMBERS
FROM TABLE 2 AREAS
54 South Asia, India
51 China
54167
5496
5412
54163
5498
54162
54165
54184
5492
5414
5417
591
5413
5415
54166
16564
Bay of Bengal
5488

Area number is added to the ultimate number in the schedules though some classes are directly based on the geographical characteristics, so the number for areas is inherent there; for example in History 954 is History of India, 973 is History for USA, as –54 and –73 are area numbers as taken from the Area Table; similarly 314 is General Statistics of Europe and 315 is General Statistics of Asia, where 4 and 5 respectively are the area numbers of Europe and Asia.

Use of Table 2 for Areas does not pose any difficulty. Whenever, a class number needs extension by some geographical area, there are sufficient instructions there in the schedules to do so. Generally, a division usually at "9" in the array is left for geographical and historical treatment of the subject:

Political Conditions
320.9

(As per instructions, this class number is to be further subdivided by the area numbers 1 to 9 from Table 2)

Political Conditions of India
320.9 + 54 (T2) = 320.954

Political Conditions in Rajasthan
320.9 + 544 (T2) = 320.954 4

Political Conditions in USA
320.973

Political conditions in Christian Countries
320.9 + 1761 (T2) = 320.917 61

Sometimes a class number itself is to be divided by the area number as per instructions there:

Constitution of Canada
342 + 71 (T2) = 342.71

Japanese Diet
328 + 52 (T2) = 328.52

Foreign Policy of Britain
327 + 41 (T2) = 327.41

Here class numbers 342, 328 and 327 have been divided by the area numbers 71, 52 and 41 respectively.

Adding Area Notation through the ss 09

Where there are no instructions but the subject of the document under classification requires the addition of area number from Table 2, then the area number is added to the class number via the ss 09, which works as a facet indicator:

Child labour in India—an economic study

331 + 09 (T1) + 54 (T2) = 331.310 954

Men Costumes in Punjab

391.1 + 09 (T1) + 5452 (T2) = 391.109 545 52

Civil Rights in Communist Countries

323.4 + 09 (T1) + 1717 (T2) = 323.409 171 7

Standard of Living in Rural Areas

339.47 + 09 (T1) + 1734 (T2) = 339.470 917 34

So, area number may be added to any class number by any of the two ways depending upon whether there is invitation or not to add from the area table.

Sometimes, an area number may be added through "0" instead of 09. For example, 920.03 –.09 Biographies by specific geographical areas.

Biographies of persons living in India

920 + 0 + 54 (T2) = 920.054

Here as per instructions, the area number 54 for India has been added to the base number 920.0

Biographies of persons living in Rajasthan

920 + 0 + 544 (T2) = 920.054 4

General libraries in USA

027 + 0 + 73 (T2) = 027.073

General libraries in Pennsylvania

027 + 0 + 748 (T2) = 027.074 8

If a subject is a study extending to two non-adjacent areas, we cannot add area numbers for both: we will have to choose one.

Democracy in India and USA

321.809 54 or 321.809 73

Education of Wokers in UK and USA

376.973 or 376.941

Here, we cannot combine both the area tables as we do in UDC. If, however, there is a relation between two different areas, then the schedules sometimes provides a mechanism to join them:

Foreign Relations between India and USA

327 + 54 (T2) + 0 + 73 (T2) = 327.540 73

Here, as per instructions, the class number 327 is to be subdivided by the first area, then 0 is to be added and to the result the area number for the second geographical area is to be added.

Similarly,

India's Foreign Policy towards Non-aligned Countries

327 + 54 (T2) + 0 + 1716 (T2) = 327.540 171 6

Trade agreements between India and USA

382.9 + 54 (T2) + 0 + 73 (T2) = 382.954 073

Migration from India to USA

304.8 + 54 (T2) + 0 + 73 (T2) = 304.854 073

Migration from Asia to developed Countries of the World

304.8 + 5 (T2) + 0 + 172 2 = 304.850 172 2

Sometimes, a geographical facet is itself inherent in the subject, i.e. it appears as a subject division in the class number:

History of India

954

General Statistics of Asia

315*

In such cases, these class numbers can further be divided like the Areas Table to provide class numbers in respect of subordinate areas.

History of Rajasthan

954.4*

General Statistics of India

315.4*

General Statistics of Rajasthan

315.44*

Class number extended by area notation can also admit a chronological subdivision. In such cases, we are only required to add the subdivision of 09 in 0901–0905 from Table 1 or by the special chronological subdivisions, if provided :

History of Mughal India

954.025

History of Rajasthan under the Mughals

954.4 + 025 (as under 954) = 954.402 5

Historical and geographical treatment of Sciences

509

History of Science in India

509.54

History of Science in British India

509.540 3

Here the chronological subdivision 03 has been taken from the history schedule of India.

---

* See also Chapter 13.

General Statistics of Asia in 19th Century

315.034

Here 034 stands for the 19th Century, as taken from the chronological table of Standard subdivisions.

Political conditions in India in 1980's

320.9 + 54 (T2) + 048 (from 09048 T1) = 320.954 048

Political conditions in Rajasthan in 1980s

320.954 404 8

Sometimes, an area may be further extended by the special subject divisions as in cases of 340 Law and 350 Public Administration:

Miscellaneous Public Law

343

Income Tax Law

343.052

Indian law of Income Tax

343 + 54 (T2) + 052 (from 343.052) = 343.540 52

Here 343 has first been divided by country (India–54) then the resulting class number has been further extended by the subject division 052 Income Tax of 343.

Similarly:

Law of Public Health

344.04

Indian Law of Public Health

344 + 54 (T2) + 04 (from 344.04) = 344.540 4

US Law of Public Health

344 + 73 (T2) + 04 (from 344.04) = 344.730 4

Prime Minister (in Cabinet form of Government)

350.003 13

Central Government of various Countries (Other than US)

354

Central Government of India

354 + 54 (T2) = 354.54

Here "54" for India from Table 2 has been added to 354 as per instructions. This can be further extended like the subdivisions of 350. For example:

Prime Minister of India

354 + 54 (T2) + 0313 (from 350.00313) = 354.540 313

Queen of Britain

354 + 41 (T2) + 0312 (from 350.00312) = 354.410 312

Separate provisions of the area table since the 17th edition, has not only allowed more details in subdivisions for various countries, but has also made possible the division of the earth and population clusters from various conceptual viewpoints. These are various physiogeographic and socio-economic regions, all shown as subdivisions of 1:

Standard of Living in Villages

339.47 + 09 (T1) + 1734 (T2) = 339.470 917 34

Atmospheric pressure in Forests

551.54 + 09 (T1) + 152 (T2) = 551.540 915 2

Here "152" is forests from the Area Table added through the ss 09.

As per instructions, each subdivision of 1 area is susceptible to be qualified by any region 3-9 from the same table. This has increased the versatility of the scheme:

Standard of Living in Indian Villages

339.47 + 09 (T1) + 1734 (T2) + 0 + 54 (T2)
= 339.470 917 340 54

Atmospheric Pressure in Indian Forests

551.54 + 09 (T1) + 9152 (T2) + 0 + 54 (T2)
= 551.540 915 205 4

Political Conditions in Communist Countries

320.9 + 1717 (T2) = 320.917 17

Political Conditions in Communist Countries of Asia

320.9 + 1717 (T2) + 0 + 5 (T2) = 320.917 170 5

Political Conditions in Christian Countries of Africa

320.9 + 1761 (T2) + 0 + 6 (T2) = 320.917 610 6

Commercial policy in British Colonies

381.3 + 09 (T1) + 1712 (T2) + 0 + 41 (T2)
= 381.309 171 204 1

Here all the subdivisions of 1 have been further extended by the area number from 3-9 via 0 which acts as a facet indicator.

* Some of the divisions may further be subdivided bv some of the other auxiliary tables. For example –174 Regions where specific racial, ethnic, national groups predominate: obviously this number is further divisible by the auxiliary Table 5:

Places where Punjabi people predominate

174 (T2) + 9142 (T5) = –174 914 2

Library buildings in the regions where Punjabi Predominates

022.33 + 1749142 = 022.331 749 142

Similarly, division –175 Regions where specific languages

---

* Please read this on second reading of the book.

predominate

Book Selection in English Speaking Countries

025.21+ 09 + 175 (T2) + 21 (T6)

= 025.210 917 521

Here area division 175 (added via 09) has been further divided by Table 6, where number for English language is 21

Hospitality of Punjabi People

395.3 + 09 (T1) + 175 (T2) + 9142 (T6)

= 395.309 175 914 2

Here Area "175" added via 09, has been extended by Table 6, where 9142 is the number for Punjabi language.

Similarly, the Area –176 can be further extended by the religions as taken from 29 and its subdivisions in Table 7:

Book Selection in Muslim Countries

025.21 + 09 (T1) + 176 (T2) + 71 (From 2971 of T6)

= 025.210 917671

Here to –176 we have added the digits following 29, in Table 7, where number for Islam is 2971.

In the schedules of many a time instructions specify that "add areas notation 3-9 from Table 2". It only means that the areas denoted by the subdivisions 1 and 2 fall outside the jurisdiction of such instructions. In such cases, we cannot add directly areas from subdivisions 1 and 2 (Table 2). If needed we can add such class numbers via the ss 09. For example, Foreign policy of non-aligned nations cannot have the following number:

327.1716

The correct number is 327 + 09 (T1) + 1716 (T2) = 327.091 716

Similarly,

Parliaments in Non-aligned nations

328 + 09 (T1) + 1716 (T2) = 328.091 716

Civil rights in Communist Countries

323.4 + 09 (T1) + 1717 = 323.409 171 7

8

USE OF TABLE 3 : Subdivisions of Individual Literatures

As the name of this auxiliary table implies, this table is exclusively meant for the main class 800 literature. This table was introduced, alongwith other tables, for the first time in the 18th edition (1971). It has since considerably eased the number building process in this class which has always been considered a problematic area. In the 19th edition, the Table 3, has been bifurcated into two tables viz, 3 and 3A, the latter is only to be used on instructions from Table 3, which in turn depends upon the instructions in the main class 800 for its use. However, in sections 808 and 809, Table 3A can be directly used with the main class number on instructions from schedules. It may be again pointed out that the subdivisions enumerated in the Table 3 and 3A are not any new or unfamiliar but have only been precipitated from the main class, especially the sections 808 and 809. What could be done earlier through the repetitious "divide like" is now done very neatly with simple "add to". These two tables have changed and made easy the mode of addition of facets. It was a step towards, making DDC more faceted and easy to operate.

The Table 3 consists of the standard subdivisions 01-07 in conformity with the Table 1. In case of the ss 08, its pristine meaning (that it carried upto the 18th edition) has been preserved, i.e., it still denotes collections and anthologies whereas for other main classes the ss 08 no more stands for anthologies etc. Hence it is now a more or less special standard subdivisions for 800 literature. The ss –08 here can be further extended by the Table 3A. The ss –09 'History, description, critical appraisal' is applicable to the body of literature regardless of form or language in which the literature is written. The ss –09 is extendable either by the period table, or by some literary viewpoints taken from Table 3A but not by both if no form of literature is given. It may be noted that period is to be taken not from the Table 1, but each language literature has its own special period (Time) tables given in the schedule of 800 (volume 2). Therefore, both the standard subdivision –08 and –09 are somewhat modified forms of the standard subdivisions here. The hard core of the table consists of the various forms of literature, which are the same for every literature irrespective of the language in which it is written:

– 1	Poetry
– 2	Drama
– 3	Fiction
– 4	Essays
– 5	Speeches
– 6	Letters
– 7	Satire and humour
– 8	Miscellaneous

Each form subdivision has further been subdivided into its various kinds and further into varieties, if any. These scopes kinds/varieties of forms have been further subdivided through a single zero, and the ss are also applicable to the form divisions through double zeroes. For example, take the form divisions. 3 Fiction:

– 3001– 3009	Standard subdivisions of Fiction
– 301– 308	Fiction of Specific Scope and Kinds
– 301	Short stories
– 306	Cartoon fiction
– 308	Specific type of fiction
– 3081	Historical and period
– 3083	Sociological, psychological, realistic
– 3084	Occupational
– 3085	Love and romance
– 3087	Adventure

Here, the subdivisions of Fiction are known as kinds of fiction, while the further division, is known as variety e.g. 3081-3087 may be termed as varieties of the specific kinds of fiction.*

31-79 is Fiction of Specific Periods.

Here 3, and for this reason any bare form division 1—8 is divisible by the period divisions specific to each language literature. Kinds of form do not admit period facet. Take, for example the case of English Fiction:

31	Fiction of Early English Period
32	Fiction of Pre-Elizabethan Period
33	Fiction of Elizabethan Period
34	Fiction of Post-Elizabethan Period
35	Fiction of Queen Anne Period
36	Fiction of Later 18th Century
37	Fiction of early 19th Century
38	Fiction of Victorian Period
39	Fiction of 20th Century

Similarly, for say, Hindi fiction the period is as follows:

31	Hindi Fiction upto 1345
32	Hindi Fiction from 1345-1645
33	Hindi Fiction from 1645-1845
34	Hindi Fiction from 1845-1895
35	Hindi Fiction from 1845-1920
36	Hindi Fiction from 1920-1940
37	Hindi Fiction after 1940

After the period division, we can further add the ss special to the main class 800 as given in Table 3.

The main class 800 has thus many facets viz. Language, Form, Period, Standard subdivision, latter being further extendable by a variety of viewpoints. In view of the multiplicity of facets, their citation order presents some complications especially when not all the facets are present. Language, form and period are the Central facets in their decreasing order of concreteness. We will discuss the various cases one by one. 9See Flow charts on Pages 95 and 96)

* *Manual on the use of the Dewey Decimal Classification: Edition 19,* Prepared by John P Comaromi and Margaret J Warren. Albany, N.Y.; Forest Press, 1982, p. 400.

I. When Language Facet is absent

Study of literature irrespective of the language falls in the sections 801 to 809. On minutely viewing, it is clear that these are the standard subdivisions (of course modified) as applied to the bare main class:

801	Philosophy and theory
802	Miscellany about literature
803	Dictionaries, encyclopaedias, etc.
805	Serial publications
806	Organisations
807	Study and teaching
808	Rhetoric and collections
809	History, description, critical appraisal of more than one literature.

Subdivisions of 801 and part of 808 have been enumerated in the schedule; some synthesis is also possible here. However, the citation order in 808.8 "Collection from more than one literature", needs some illustrations. The citation formula is

Base number 808.8 + Form + Period (From Table 1)

Collections from 20th Century Literature (Regardless of Form)

808.8001 – .8005 Collections from specific period.

As per instructions here, we are to add to the base number 808.800, the number following 090 in 0901–0905 from Table 1 (of standard subdivisions). Their number for 20th Century is 0904, thus the digit following 090 is "4" only. Hence the class number is

808.800 + 4 = 808.800 4

Similarly:

Collection of 16th Century Literature

808.800 + 31 (from 09031 Table 1) = 808.800 31

Selections from literature of 1990's

808.800 = + 49 (from 09049 Table 1) = 808.800 49

A Collection of Poetry

808.81

Collections from Poetry of 1990's

808.81 + 0 + 49 = 808.810 49

808.81 is collections from poetry. This number is an asterisked number. As per instructions given under 808.81 – 808.88 we have added to the 808.81 the notation for period as explained there. Again the period has been taken from general period table viz. Table 1 of standard subdivisions. As a rule, when no language is given, the period is to be taken from the Table 1 of standard subdivisions.

It may be noted that period division cannot be added to the collections of some specific forms of literature displaying a specific kind or displaying some specific feature.

Collection of Epic Poetry of 20th Century

808.81 + 3 = 808.813

(No period has been added)

Similarly,

Collection of 20th Century Drama on Social Themes

808.829 + 355 (T3A) = 808.829 355

The notation 355 has been added from Table 3A, as per instructions under 808.829. No period division for 20th Century can be added as there are no instructions to do so.

II. When Language is Present

Literature of specific languages is classed in 810—890, and the language makes the first facet in the citation order. Procedure for building a co-extensive class number for any language literature has been explained in the schedule on pages 1398-1400. It may be stated as follows in a simplified manner.

Combination of main class digit 8', and the language constitutes the compound facet, which is termed as the base. It is the base to which all other facets are added in an ordained order. Base numbers for almost all the languages have been enumerated and specifically indicated. For some minor or obscure languages, base number can be built with the help of language number taken from Table 6 Languages.

For example:

891.99.	Literature in other Indo-European languages.
891.991	Albanian
891.892	Armenian
891.993–.998	Others

Here the instruction reads: Add to 891.99 the number following 9199 in Language notation 91993–91998 from Table 6, e.g. Hittide 891.998. In this way, the class number for Tocharian language literature is 891.994. This however is not the base number but the final class number as no other facet is admissible to such a number.

To the available base number in the schedule, we add the facets in the following order:

> Base number + Form + Period + ss 08 or 09 (Subject/ viewpoint from Table 3A) (See flow charts)

It is obvious that in a given literary work all the above facets may not be present all the times. Form facet is to be taken from Table 3. General instructions have been provided in the main class 800 to use the Table 3, and this table is invariably needed to build class number for titles having both the specified language and form. Whenever the Table 3 is to be used such base numbers are marked with an asterisk*. Even for major literatures readymade class number adding the form facet have been enumerated. For example:

821	English Poetry
822	English Drama
827	English Satire and Humour
861	Spanish Poetry
862	Spanish Drama
863	Spanish Fiction
864	Spanish Essays
865	Spanish Speeches
866	Spanish Letters
867	Spanish Satire and Humour
868	Spanish miscellaneous writings

Instructions to use the Table 3 and to construct a class number have been explained in a programmatic manner preceding the divisions in Table 3, viz., pp. 387-388 (Volume 1). These instructions have made the facet structure quite transparent, though the instructions do not make a very easy reading mostly due to multiplicity of facets.

In case of individual authors the standard subdivisions and their further extension by standard subdivisions and Table 3A is not admissible. Hence the books by and on an individual literary author get the same number. For example:

A critical study of John Keats' Poetry
(He was an English Poet of early 19th Century)
82 (Base) + 1 (Form Poetry) + 7 (Period from pp. 1403-4)
= 82 + 1 + 7 = 821.7
(Here we cannot add the ss for criticism)

Similarly, a study of plot construction in the novels of Thomas Hardy will get the class number as follows:

82 (Base) + 3 (Form, Fiction from Table 3) + 8
= 82 + 3 + 8 = 823.8

Here, the critical element "Plot Construction" will have to be ignored. Any work of fiction by Hardy, or any work on Hardy, as a fiction writer will get the class number 823.8, and the various Victorian novelists such as Hardy, George Eliot, Thackery, Dickens, Mrs Gaskell could only be differentiated through Book Numbers. However, the works on and by an individual writer can further be divided on the analogy of the classification of the works on and by William Shakespeare 822.33. This, however, is beyond the scope of the present work.

III. In case the Form is absent, the citation formula takes the following order:

Base Number + 080 + Table 3A (No period)
Base Number + 0900 + Period for that Specific literature
+ Table 3A for viewpoint or theme
Collection of Hindi literature on love theme.
891.43 + 080 + 354 (T3A) = 891.430 803 54
Collection of Hindi Literature on Tragedy
891.43 + 080 + 16 (T3A) = 891.430 801 6
Critical Study of Characters in English Literature
82 + 09 + 27 (T3A) = 820.927

History of 20th Century English Literature
82 + 0900 + 91 = 820.900 91

In the facet formula, the third facet is the time period in which the author flourished as a writer. It may be noted that in case of a specific language literature, the period is not to be taken from the ss 09 of Table 1. For every language literature, special period divisions enumerating epochs of that particular literature have been given in the schedules at the beginning of each language literature. For example, for American literature, the Period Table as given under 810 is :

1 Colonial period 1607–1776
2 Post-Revolutionary period 1776–1830
3 Middle 19th century 1830–1861
4 Later 19th century 1861–1900
5 Twentieth century

52 Early, 1900–1945
54 Later, 1945 –

It is specially to be noted about the period table that in case the literature in that language is written in more than one country, then different period tables are given for each major country. For example, for French literature different period tables exist for Asian and African countries, for Belgium, for Canada and of course for France. It is obvious, as each country has different epochs in its literary history of that language. For instance, for French language literature period Table for French is :

For Asian and African Countries

1 To 1960
2 Later 20th Century, 1960.

For Belgium

1 Early Period to 1830
2 19th Century, 1830-1900
3 20th Century.
32 Early, 1900-1945
34 Later, 1945 –

For Canada

3 Colonial period to 1867
4 Later 19th Century, 1867-1900
5 20th Century
52 Early, 1900-1945
54 Later, 1945 –

For France

1 Early period to 1400
2 15th century, 1400-1500
3 16th century, 1500-1600
4 Classical period, 1600-1715
5 18th century, 1715-1789
6 Revolution and Empire, 1789-1815
7 Constitutional monarchy, 1815-1848
8 Later 19th century, 1848-1900
9 1900 –
91 20th century
912 Early, 1900-1945
914 Later, 1945 -

After adding the period division, the ss may be added with only one zero. Detailed instructions have been provided to give step by step guidance. The period division is further extendable by the standard subdivisions as taken from 1001-1009. Here the ss begins only with a single zero, as per rule. If needed, these ss especially 08 and 09 may further be extended by the viewpoint Table 3A. For example.

Collection of Victorian Poetry. (It means it is English Poetry of late nineteenth century).

Base (English Language Literature)	82
Poetry (Form, Table 3)	1
Victorian Period (pp. 1403-4 of Vol. 2)	8
Collection (as Instructed under 11-19 Table 3)	08

From Table 3. We have added to the period division the number following 10 in 1001-1009, and Collection is 1008

Hence the complete class number is

82 + 1 + 8 + 08 = 821.808

Similarly:

Critical appraisal of Victorian fiction

82 + 3 + 8 + 09 = 823.809

Social themes in Victorian Fiction

For critical appraisal of Victorian fiction. we have 823.809. Since 08 and 09 are further extendable by Table 3A, so we can add to the result the appropriate notation for social themes in Table 3A which is 355. Hence the complete class number is

823.809 + 355 = 823.809 355

Again

Critical study of plots in Post-War American novels:

81 (Base) + 3 (Form) + 54 (Period)
+ 09 (Critical appreciation, Table 3)
+ 24 (Plot, Table 3A)
= 81 + 3 + 54 + 09 + 24 = 813.540 924

Some graded examples will help to clarify:

American Literature

810

Dictionary of American Literature

81+ 03 = 810.3

(Note, Base for American Literature is 81)

International Conference on American Literature

81 + 0601 (T1) = 810.601

All India Conference on American Literature

81 + 060 (T1) + 54 (T2) = 810.605 4

(We have added –54 from Table 2 to the base number 060 from Table 1. This has been done as per instructions under the ss —0603–9)

History of the American Literature of the Colonial Period

81 + 0900 + 1 = 810.900 1

(Here 1 has been added from the period Table for the American literature given at page 1401)

History of 20th Century American Literature

81+ 0900 + 5 (p. 1401, vol. 2) = 810.900 5

History of American Literature for Children

81 + 09 + Notation for Children in Table 3A

= 81 + 09 + 9282 = –810.992 82

History of Realism in American Literature

81+ 09 + 12 (T3A, Realism) = 81 + 09 + 12 = 810.912

American Poetry

81 + 1 = 811

Dictionary of American Poetry

81 + 1003 (T3) = 811.003

All India Conference on American Poetry

81 + 10060 (T3 & T1) + 54 (T2) = 811.006 054

History of American Poetry

81 + 1009 (T3) = 811.009

American Epic Poetry

81 + 103 (T3) = 811.03

Dictionary of American Epic Poetry

81 + 103 (T3) + 03 (T1) = 811.030 3

All India Conference on American Epic Poetry

81 + 103 (T3) + 06054 (T1, T2) = 811.030 605 4

History of American Epic Poetry

81 + 103 + 09 = 811.030 9

History of Realism in American Epic Poetry

Though in the subject here, period viz 20th Century exists, but as per provisions for the kind of poetry, we cannot add it; so we will have to ignore the period, and treat it as if it is the history of American Epic poetry respective of time = 81 + 103 + 09 = 811.030 9

Literary works without language and form

Collection of 20th Century Literature

808.8 Collection from more than one Literature

808.8001-.8005 Collection from Specific periods

As per instructions, we are to add to the base number 808.800 the number following 090 in ss notation 0901-0905 from Table 1 = 808.800 + 4 = 808.800 4

The readers may be again reminded here that the period has been taken from the general period table viz the Table 1 Collection of literature on Social Themes:

808.801–.803 Collections displaying specific features.

Here, we are to add to the base number, 808.80 notation 1-3 from Table 3A. In Table 3A the notation for social themes is 355. Hence the required class number is

808.80 + 355 = 808.803 55

Collection of Epic Poetry

(No language and period)

808.81 Collection of Poetry

808.812–.818 Collection of Specific kind of Poetry

As per instructions here we are to add to the base number 808.81, then number following 10 in 102–108 of Table 3 Subdivisions of Individual literature. The notation for Epic Poetry is 103. So, as per instructions we are to add "3" to the base 808.81

808.81 + 3 = 808.813

Critical Appraisal of the Romanticism in the 19th Century English Poetry

821 + 7 + 09 + 145 = 821.709 145

Portrayals of Children in Victorian English Fiction (Period is later 19th Century: the Victorian Period)

823.7+ 09 + 352 + 054 (Table 7) = 823.709 352 054

Account of London in English Drama of Queen Anne Period

822 + 5 (period) + 09 + 32 (Place) from Table 3A

= 822.50932 + 421 (London)

Specific Place from Area Table 2 = 822.50932 + 421

(Table 2) = 822.509 324 21

Depiction of India in Victorian Fiction

82 + 3 + 8 + 09 + 32 + 54 (Table 2) = 823.809 325 4

Collection of English Literature written by Negroes

82 + 08 + 0 + 8 (From Table 3A) + 036 (Table 5)
= 820.808 036

20th century French Literature – A critical appraisal
84 + 0900 + 91 (For 20th Century) = 840.900 91

Romanticism in English Poetry
82 + 1009 (Table 3) + 145 (Table 3A) = 821.009 145

Plot in 17th Century Spanish Novel
86 + 3 + 3 (Period) + 09 + 24 (Table 3A) = 863.309 24

Description of Women in 20th Century English Novel
82 + 3 + 91 + 09 + 352 (Table 3A) + 042 (Table 7)
= 823.910 935 204 2

Collection of German Language Literature written by Englishmen
83 + 08 + 0 + 8 (Table 3A) + 21 (Table 5)
= 830.808 21

Collection of German Language Literature by Jews
83 + 08 + 0 + 8 + 924 (Table 5) = 830.808 924

Collection of German Language literature by Afro-Asian writers
83 + 08 + 0 + 9 (Table 3 A) + 17165 (From Table 2)
= 830.809 171 65

Depiction of Indian religions in English Literature
82 + 09 + 4 (Table 3A) + 294 (From the schedules 001 – 999) = 820.942 94

A critical study of plot in Hindi Novels of Early 20th Century
891.433 + 09 + 24 (T3A) = 891.433 092 4

Contributions to Hindi Literature by Bengalis—A critical study (no form, no period)
891.43 + 09 (ss from Table 3)
+ 8 (Literature for and by various specific racial ethnic, national groups from table 3A)

As per instructions, 8 is to be further subdivided by Table 5, where the notation for Bengali people is 9144

Hence the complete number is
891.43098 + 9144 (Table 5) = 891.430 989 144

Contribution to Hindi literature by Bengalis after 1940
891.430 900 7

Contributions of Bengalis to Hindi Poetry (No period)
891.43 + 1009 + Table 3A = 891.431009 + 8 + 9144 (Table 5) = 891.431 009 891 44

Contribution of Bengalis to Hindi Poetry of Post 1940 era

891.43 + 1 (From) + 7 (Period) + 09 (ss) + Table 3A+
Table 5 = 891.43 + 1 (From) + 7 (period) + 09 (ss) + 8 (by various national, ethnic groups, Table 3A) + 9144 (For Bengalis from Table 5)
= 891.431 709 891 44

Hindu Religion in British Fiction
823.009 + 4 (Table 3A) + 2945 (by 001-999)
= 823.009 429 45

Hindu Religion in 20th Century British Fiction
823 + 9 (Period) + 09 + 4 + 2945 = 823.909 429 45

Collection of Hindi Literature for Children
891.43 + 080 (Table 3) + 9282 (Table 3A)
= 891.430 809 282

Collection of Hindi Poetry for Children
891.43 + 10080 (T3)+9282 (T3A) = 891.431 008 092 82

Collection of Modern Hindi Poetry for Children
891.43 + 1 + 7 (Period) + 08 + (Table 3) + 9282 (T3A)
= 891.431 708 928 2

Critical study of Women Novelists of Victorian Period
823 + 8 (Period) + 09 + 9287 = 823.809 928 7

The reader may be again reminded that the elements from Table 3, or 3A can only be added on instructions. Where a number admits notation from Table 3, such a number is marked with an asterisk. Where there is no asterisk, the number cannot be extended further. For example,

Old Low Germanic Literature
839.1

If we have old Law Germanic Poetry even then the class number is 839.1

Anthology of Pali Literature 891.3

Anthology of Pali Poetry 891.3

(Here no other facet is admissible)

Let us take some more examples:

Stream of consciousness in 20th Century English Novel
82 + 3 + 91 + 09 + 25 = 823.910 925

Anthology of French poems composed by Indians
(Here there is no period divisions)

Base number for French Literature	84
Collection of Poetry	1008

For Indians, as per instruction, the number is to be taken from 93—99 of Table 3A. Here 9 is the base which is to be further synthesised

Flow Chart of Literature

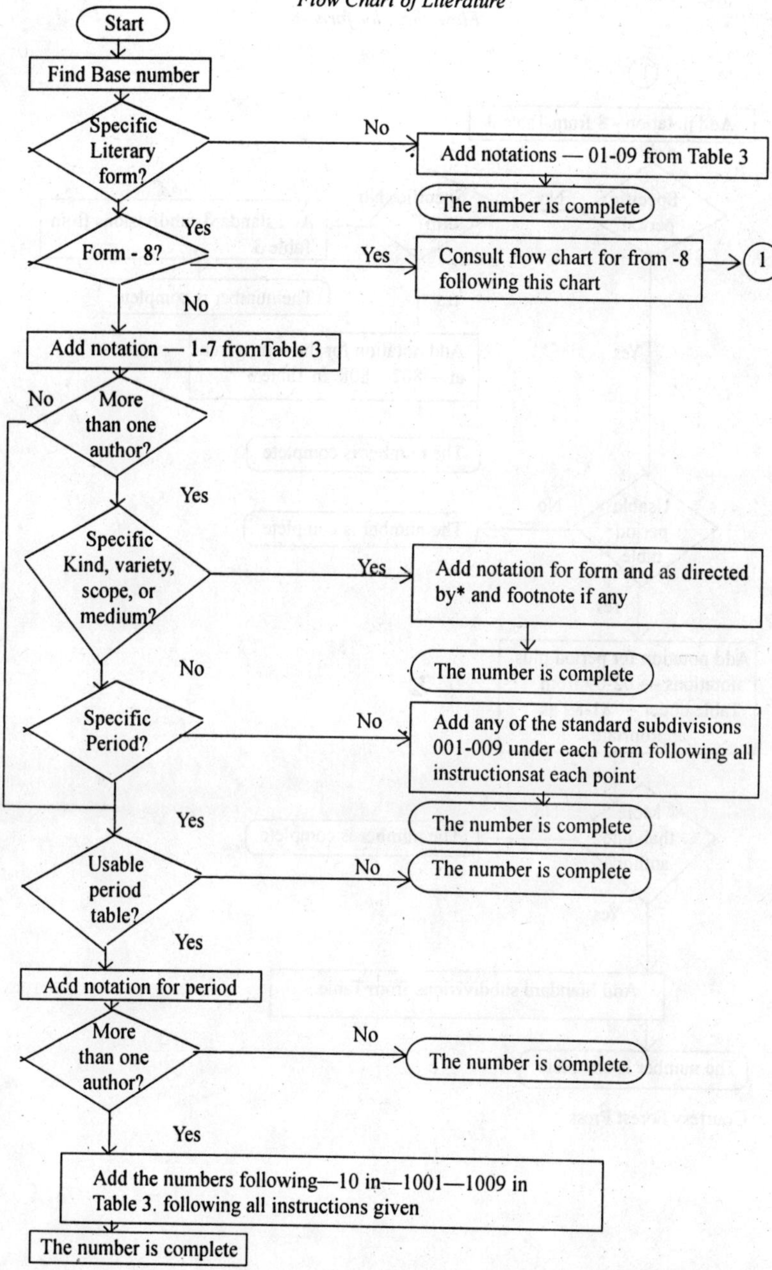

Flow chart for form -8

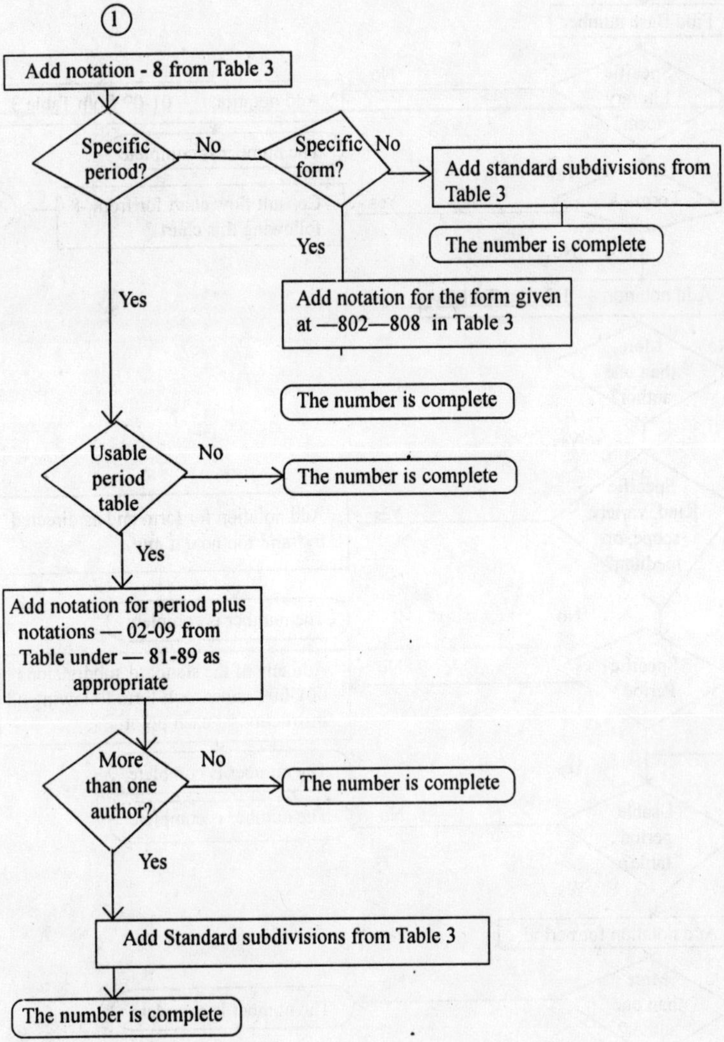

Courtesy Forest Press

from Table 2, thus, the number for Indian is

9 + 54 = 954

Making 10080 as the base, we add to it the number for Indians:

84 + 1008 + 0 + 954 = 841.008 095 4

Collection of Hindi Lyrical Love Poetry

891.43 + 103 + 08+ 354 = 891.431 030 835 4

Critical appraisal of Punjabi Satirical Poetry written by the writers living in Canada

891.42 + 107 (T3) + 09 (as under·-1-8(T3)
+9 (from 93-99 T3A) + 71 (T2) = 891.421 070 997 1

Collection of English Literature written by Children

Base = 82

Collection = 08 (Table 3)

Here we have the instructions to go to Table 3A where number of children writer is 9282:

82 + 08 + 9282= 820.892 82

Critical Appraisal of Hindi short stories written by Punjabis

Base number for Hindi Fiction =891.43

Short Stories (T3) =301

Finding instructions, we go to instructions under —1—8 specific Forms page 390 (Vol. I)

Critical Appraisal 09

Literature for and by various specific racial ethnic national groups 8

8 is further to be extended by notations 03-99 from Table 5, where number for Punjabis is 9142

Hence the complete number is

891.43 + 301 + 09 + 8 + 9142 = 891.433 010 989 142

Use of Table 3 in other Main Classes

Table 3, specifically 3A also finds use in the class 792

Theatre—for the obvious relation between theatre and literature

792.0909 Special aspects (of Theatre)

The instruction reads "add notations 1-3 from Table 3A to base number 792.0909 . . . "

Theatrical dialogues

792.0909 + 26 (T3A) = 792.090 926

Treatment of social Themes in Theatre

792.0909 + 355 (T3A) = 792.090 935 5

Since 792.1 - 792.8 can further be divided by

792.04–.09 so the table 3A is also applicable here.

Dialogues in a comedy play

792.230 909 26

Social themes in comedies

792.230 909 355

9

USE OF TABLE 4 : Subdivisions of Individual Languages of 400 Languages Schedule

This, one of the simplest tables to use, is exclusively used for the Main Class 400 Linguistics. If need be, it may further be extended by the Table 6 languages. The table 4 enlists linguistic elements and problems.

Main Class digit 4 and the language number taken together make the base, and the base numbers for all the major languages have been enumerated. The base number is further extendable by Table 4 and if further need be by Table 6. The facet formula that emerges out is:

Base number + Table 4 + Table 6

Whenever Table 4 or Table 6 is to be used, sufficient instructions guide us by marking the base number with an asterisk* :

Grammar of English Language
Base number for English = 42
Grammar (Table 4) = 5
= 425

A study of words of Sanskrit Language
Base number for Sanskrit 491.2
(Words Table 4) 81
491.281

Hindi Primer (reader) for English speaking people
491.43 + 864 (T4) + 21 (T6) = 491.438 642 1

Bilingual Dictionaries

The DDC is able to provide very precise class numbers for bilingual dictionaries. Here the language in which the words are given form the base number: to the base number 3 Dictionaries (from Table 4), is added and to the resulting class number the language number for the language in which meanings are given is added as taken from Table 6. Thus the formula is:

Base number + 3 (Table 4) + Table 6

For example, take "Sanskrit–German Dictionary". Here Sanskrit forms the base number, as the words are given in Sanskrit.

491.2 + 3 (T4) + Number for German from Table 6
= 491.2 + 3 + 31 = 491.233 1

Similarly, the class number for German–Sanskrit Dictionary will be

43 + 3 + 912 (T6) = 433.912

(Here 43 is the base number for German language and 912 the number for Sanskrit language as taken from Table 6).

Similarly:

Russian-Punjabi Dictionary

491.7 + 3 + 9142 = 491.739 142

English-French Dictionary

42 + 3 + 41 = 423.41

Table 4 may also be supplemented by the Table 6 in many other cases also:

Use of English words in Hindi Language

It is the study of Hindi Language so it will form the base number. For foreign elements, we have 24 in Table 4 which is further extendable by Table 6:

491.43 + 24 + Number for English from Table 6
= 491.43 + 24 + 21 = 491.432 421

Similarly,

French Phrases in English language

42 + 24 (T4) + 41 (T6) = 422.441

English primer for Hindi Speaking learners

42 + 864 + 9143 = 428.649 143

It may further be noted that in the schedule of Main Class 400 Languages, class number for all the known languages do not exist, but the base number for such unenumerated languages can be crystallised through the use of Table 6. Instructions to add from Table 6 exist in such cases. For example:

Tocharian Language

(It is a member of Baltic family of Languages and the class number for it has not been given specifically).

At 491.9, we have Baltic and other Languages. Some Languages have been enumerated, 491.993 –.998 are other languages. Instructions say that to obtain the class number for any of the other Languages, we are to add to 491.99, the number following 9199 in 91993 – 91998 from Table 6. The number in Table 6 for Tocharian Languages is 91994.

Thus the number for Tocharian Languages is:

491.99 + 4 = 491.994

Similarly for Egyptian Languages (It belongs to the family of Hamitic and Chad Languages whose class number is 493). As per instructions at 493, the class number for Egyptian Languages is:

493 + 1 = 493.1

Similarly for Mongolic Languages (which belong to Altic Languages family) Base number is 494. The class number thus is:

494 + 2 = 494.2

Some other Class numbers illustrating the use of Main Class 400

English Dialects

427.9

Indian English

427.9 + 54 (T2) = 427.954

Pakistani English

427.954 9

(Here 427.9 has been subdivided by area table)

English Slang

427.09

10

USE OF TABLE 5: Racial, Ethnic and National Groups

This table enumerates people based upon their Racial or Ethnic or National origins. In the 18th edition, the use of this table was very limited as it could be used only on invitation, but in the 19th edition through the ss –089 its application has been universalised. It means that a subject can be treated among groups of people characterised by their national, racial or ethnic origin, even if there are no instructions in the schedules: Its use is very simple: where there are instructions in the schedules we are simply to add the notation from Table 5 to the designated base number in the schedule.

Psychology of Negroes

For Psychology of Specific racial and ethnic groups, we have the class number

155.84

Under this class number, we have the instructions that to the base number 155.84, we have to add the number from the Table 5, where the number for Negroids is –036. The full class number, therefore, is

155.84 + 036 = 155.840 36

Similarly,

Psychology of Swedes

155.84 + 397 = 155.843 97

Class Numbers for some of the lesser known religions are obtainable with the application of Table 5

299 Other Religions

299.1–.4 of Indo–European, Semitic, North African, North and West Asians, Dravidian origin.

"Add Racial, Ethnic, National Groups Notation 91–94 from Table 5 to base Number 29. . ."
For example :

Mithraism (It is a religion of Iranians)

29 + 915 = 299.15

Druidism (It is religion of Celts)

29 + 916 = 299.16

Similarly, 299.68 is also further divisible by the Table 5 to get the number for religions of specific tribes.

Another officially invited use occurs at 305.8 Social Structure of Racial Ethnic and National Groups :

A Social Study of Bengalis

(Bengalis are a Linguistic Ethinc Group)

305.8 is the base number to which the notation for Bengalis is to be added from Table 5, as per instructions:

305.8 + 9144 (T5) = 305.891 44

Encyclopedia of Jewish Society

305.8 + 924 + 03 (T1) = 305.892403

Another inevitable use of Table 5 occurs at 641.592 Ethnic Cookery. Here instructions exist to add to the above base the notation from Table 5 for the Cookery of corresponding racial, ethnic or national groups.

Scientific Principles of Punjabi method of preparing food

641.592 + 9142 + 015 (T1) = 641.592 914 2 015

Another official use of the Table 5 is made at 784.76 Songs of ethnic and cultural groups, which is in fact a part of 784.4 Folk Songs. Under 784.76 there is instruction to "add Racial Ethnic, National Groups notation 01–99 from Table 5 to base number 784.76".

It may be noted that Class number for songs of ethnic and cultural groups in the United States and Canada is already enumerated at 784.75, therefore US and Canadian culture group do not fall at 784.76

Punjabi Folk Songs

784.76 + 9142 = 784.769 142

Folk Songs of Indian Gypsies

784.76 + 91497 = 784.769 149 7

Folk Songs of Dutchs

784.76 + 3931 = 784.763 931

Folk Songs of North Americans

784.75,

Not 784.76 + 1 = 784.761

Some of the numbers in Table 5 are further divisible by Table 2. For example in Table 5, the subdivision –68 Spanish Americans is further divisible by national groups of Spanish Americans by the addition of notation 7–8 from Table 2 to the base number –68.

Columbian Peoples –68 + –861 = –68861

Bolivians

– 68 + – 84 = – 6884

Therefore, the class number for "Folk Songs of Bolivians is :

784.76 + 68 (T5) + 84 (T2) = 784.766 884

Similarly, National Groups of Arabs are obtainable by the addition of area notation 5–6 from Table 2 to the base number –927.

Libyans

– 927 (T5) + – 612 (T2) = 927612

Therefore, the class number for Libyan Society is :

305.8 + –927612 = 305.892 761 2

Sometimes the area from Table 2 is added through the addition of zero as a facet indicator e.g. –96073 United States blacks. For "US blacks in Canada" the notation may be obtained by adding area number for Canada to the above base, but through the addition of a zero e.g.

– 96073071

Though the instructions are not explicit, the above method can be generalised, e.g.

Indians in U.S.

– 91411073

Bengalis in England

– 9144 (T5) + 0 + 42 (T2) – 9144042

Brazilians in U.S.A

– 698 + 0 + 73 = – 698073

Nepalis in India

– 91495 + 0 + 54 = – 91495054

Above generalization stands approved by the note given under 305.8 where instructions are provided to study a racial, ethnic, or national group of people in some countries of the world. Here area is added to the notation from Table 5 through a 0 (zero).

Social Study of Indians in the United States.

Indians here are a national group.

The base class number is 305.8

As per instruction, to this base, number for Indians is added from Table 5.

Social Study of Indians

305.8 + 91411 = 305.891 411

For Indians in U.S.A. to the resultant class number, add 0 and then the area number for USA as taken from Table 2.

305.891411 + 0 + 73 (T2) = 305.891 411 073

Similarly

Social Study of Nepalis in India

305.8 + 91495 (T5) + 0 + 54 (T2) = 305.891 495 054

Folk Songs of Libyans

784.76 + 927612 = 784.769 276 12

Use of T5 through the ss – 089

Apart from these, other situations demanding the use of Table 5, can be dealt through the use of ss –089

Child Labour among Indians

331.31 + 089 (Table 1) + 91411 (Table 5)

= 331.310 899 141 1

Indian Handicraftsmen in England

745.5 + 089 + 91411 + 0 + 42 = 745.508 991 411 042

Reading Habits of Indians

028.9 + 089 + 91411 = 028.908 991 411

Reading Habits of Indians in England

028.908991411 + 0 + 42 = 028.908 991 411 042

World History of Jews

909.04 + 924 (From Table 5) = 909.049 24

Similarly

History of Punjabis in the World

909.04 + 9142 = 909.049 142

Period subdivisions of World History as given under 909.1–909.8 (p. 1437, v. 2) can also be added with a zero as facet indicator.

World History of Punjabis in the 19th Century.

909.04 + 9142 (T5) + 0 + 8 (from 909.8)

= 909.049 142 08

World History of Celts in 20th Century

909.04 + 916 (T5) + 82 = 909.049 168 2

Collected biographies of Jews

920.0092 + 924 (T5) = 920.009 292 4

Collected biographies of Punjabis

920.0092 + 9142 (T5) = 920.009 291 42

Collected biographies of Celts

920.0092 + 916 (T5) = 920.009 291 6

Education of Punjabis in Canada .

371.97 + 9142 (T5) + 0 + 71 (T2) = 371.979 142 071

Education of Eskimos in U.S.A.

371.97 + 97 (T5) + 073 = 371.979 707 3

Sinhalese migrant labour in New York State

331.63 + 9148 (T5) + 0 + 747(T2)

= 331.639 148 074 7

Migrant Labour of South Asian Origin in Canada

331.63 + 914 (T5) + 0 + 71 (T2) = 331.639 140 71

Jew Migrant Labour in U.S.A.

331.63 + 924 (T5) + 0 + 73 (T2) = 331.639 240 73

Migrant Labour of Tanzanian Origin in North America

331.63 + 96 (T5) + 78 (Following 6 in Table 2, where Tanzania is 678) + 0 + 7 (T2)

= 331.639 678 07

Similarly

Migrant Labour of Nigerian Origin in Mexico

331.63 + 96 + 69 + 0 + 72

= 331.639 669 072

11

USE OF TABLE 6: Languages

Whenever any subject is further divisible by a language facet the notation from Table 6 is added to the specified base number. (Previously, this was done through divide like 420–490 instructions). Provision of a separate table enlisting almost all the languages has eased the process of synthesis; and made possible the detailed enumeration of many lesser known languages not hitherto easy.

Table 6 is to be used to supplement a number from the schedules or even from the Tables only on invitation. For example, this division of 030 General Encyclopaedias has been on broad languages group, which further can be sorted into individual languages by the use of Table 6. For example :

036 Encyclopaedias in Spanish and Portuguese

For any specific language encyclopaedia in this language group, one has to add to 03 the number for the particular language in 61–69 in Table 6, as per instructions:

Spanish Encyclopaedia

03 + 61= 036.1

Papiamento Language Encyclopaedia

03 + 68 = 036.8

Similarly, 039 is Encyclopaedia in other languages (not provided for in 031—038). Class numbers for other encyclopaedias are to be obtained by adding language notation 2–9 from Table 6 to base number 039.

Vishv Kosh (Encyclopaedia in Hindi Language)

039 + 9143 = 039.914 3

General Encyclopaedia in Japanese

039 + 956 = 039.956

Similarly, class numbers for various translations of the Bible are also got by the device of Table 6:

220. 5 Modern versions and translations of the Bible.

220.53 – .59 Bible in other languages.

For different languages, we are asked to add the number for the corresponding language from Table 6 to the specified base 220.5

Bible in Hindi

220.5 + 9143 = 220.591 43

Bible in German

220.5 + 31 = 220.531

Though the Table 6 has been used at a fairly large number of places in the schedules but the main classes 400 Linguistics and 800 Literature appear to be intrinsic fields of its applications. In these two fields, the use of this Table has already been discussed and illustrated while dealing with the use of Table 3 and Table 4 respectively.

In the Main class 400 Linguistics all the major languages have been enumerated with the exception of some lesser known languages. But the Table 6 contains almost an exhaustive list of all the known languages. Therefore, the class numbers for these unenumerated languages can be obtained by the use of Table 6 on instructions.

For example:

470 Italic languages

479 Other Italic Languages

to be obtained by adding to the base number 479 the number following 79 in 794–799 in Table 6.

Linguistic study of Faliscan language

Faliscan language is one of the Italic languages, which has not been enumerated under 470–478. Therefore, it will obviously go to 479. In the Table 6 under –79 and its parts, we see that the notation for Faliscan language is 794. Following the above instructions, the class number for Faliscan language is:

479 + 4 (from 794 of T6) = 479.4

(We have added to 479 the digits following 79, which is "4").

Similar instructions appear at 491.993 – .998, 493, 494, 495.92 –.95, 496, 497 and 498.

Again take Tupi language (It is a South American native language). Its class number is:

498 + 3 = 498.3

The use of Table 6 in conjunction with Table 4 for bilingual dictionaries in 400 has already been amply demonstrated in the chapter on the use of Table 4.

Similarly in 800 Literature Schedule some of the languages not enumerated can be obtained by the use of Table 6. The use here is just analogous to its use in 400 linguistics.

For example, 893 Hamitic and Chad Literature.

(Here particular language literature in this family of languages is to be obtained by adding to the base number 893 the number following 93 in 931–937 in Table 6).

Egyptian Literature

893 + 1 = 893.1

(Since 931 is Egyptian language in Table 6, and the digit coming after 93 is "1").

Similarly

Somali Literature

893 + 5 = 893.5

(Since notation for Somali language is 935 in Table 6)

Another inevitable use of the Table 6 is at 372.65 Foreign language skill in Elementary Schools.

Teaching of specific foreign languages in elementary schools is got by adding to the base 372.65 the relevant notation from Table 6.

Hindi as a second language in elementary schools

372.65 + 9143 (T6) = 372.659 143

German as a foreign language in Elementary Schools

372.65 + 31 = 372.653 1

Class numbers derived from 372.65 can further be synthesised by adding facets enumerated under 372.3 —372.8

Curriculun in German as second language in elementary schools

372.65 + 31 (T6) + 043 (as under 372.3 – 372.8)
= 372.653 104 3

Teaching of German as second language in Elementary Schools

372.6531 + 044 = 372.653 104 4

Some more examples on the use of Table 6

A General Periodical in Hindi

059 + 9143 = 059.914 3

A General Periodical in Romanian Language

05 + 591 = 055.91

A General Periodical in Spanish

05 + 61 = 056.1

A French Language Encyclopaedïa

03 + 41 = 034.1

English Proverbs

398.9 + 21 = 398.921

Spanish Proverbs

398.9 + 61 = 398.961

Hindi Proverbs

398.9 + 9143 = 398.991 43

Sanskrit Calligraphy

745.6199 + 912 = 745.619 991 2

Calligraphy in Artificial Languages

745.6199 + 9999 = 745.619 999 99

12

USE OF TABLE 7 : Persons

This table enlists persons by their social, psychological or some other individual characteristics such as health, age, marital status and lastly and largely by their profession. The notation slice 01–08 denotes the former group of persons; while the subject specialists have been denoted mnemonically with the general schedules by the whole gamut of the table viz 1–9:

1	Persons occupied with Philosophy etc.
2	Persons occupied with Religion
	....
5	Persons occupied with Pure Sciences.

and so on. The persons occupied with Generalia disciplines such as bibliographers, library scientists, journalists have been placed at 09.

Brief introduction to apply this table precedes the enlisting of persons (pp. 432–452 Vol. 1). This table can be used on instructions given in the main schedules or in various tables; or it can be applied of its own through the ss –088. This table is used when the development, practice or state of the subject is studied in relation to a specified group of persons. In the 17th edition such a versatility was mostly not possible, but in some cases, it was obtained through divide-like 001–999 or smaller parts of the schedules. This separate table has eased the process and carried it to more depths. For example take

Social stratification of Baptists

It is a subject of sociology, where social stratification is placed at 305, and here the social stratification of various religious groups is placed at

305.6. Here as per instructions, we are to add to the base 305.6 the number following 2 in 21–29 from Table 7. The notation for Baptists in Table 7 is 261, so we will add 61 to the designated base:

305.6 + 61 = 305.661 is the appropriate class number.

This derived class number may further be subdivided by Area table (T2) through the facet indicator 0 (zero):

Social stratification of Baptists in India

305.661 + 0 + 54 = 305.661 054

Social stratification of Baptists in Europe

305.661 + 0 + 4 = 305.661 04

Another official invitation to use the Table 7 is extended at 390.4 Customs of people of various specific occupations. It is to be further subdivided by the Table 7 notation from 09 to 99. For example:

Customs of Librarians

390.4 + 092 = 390.4 092

Customs of Historians

390.4 + 97 = 390.497

where 092 and 97 are the numbers for librarians and historians respectively in Table 7.

Similarly, 704 Special topics of general applicability in fine and decorative arts can be extended by the Table 7 notation from 04 to 87.

Buddhists as Artists

704 + 2447 = 704.244 7

where 2447 is the notation for Buddhism in Table 7.

Art works by Scientists

704 + 5 = 704.5

174 is Economic, Professional, Occupational Ethics.

Ethics of some of the professions have been enumerated, e.g.

174.2 Ethics of Medical Profession

174.3 Ethics of Lawyers, etc.

Ethics for all other professions have been placed at 174.9, and we have been asked to get the individual class number for ethics of rest of the professions by adding notation 09–99 from Table 7. For example:

Ethics of Librarianship

174.9 + 092 = 174.909 2

Here 092 has been taken from Table 7, where it means "persons occupied with library and information Sciences"

Ethics of Historians

174.9 + 97 = 174.997*

In addition to its invited use at various places in the main schedules, the use of Table 7 has also been suggested in various ancilliary tables. For instance in Table 1 (Standard sub-divisions) "024 works for specific types of users" is further extendable by Table 7 for works specifying the type of user:

Library Classification for Philosophers

025.42 is classification (and for a subject of a specific type of users, we have the ss 024, which as per instructions is further divisible by Table 7. For Philosophers we have the notation 11 in Table 7). Thus the complete class number is:

025.42 + 024 + 11 = 025.420 241 1

Philosophy for Librarians

100 + 024 (T1) + 092 (T7) = 102.4092

Similarly

Mathematics for Engineers

= Mathematics for specific type of users

510 + 24 = 510.24

For Engineer, we have the notation 62 in Table 7.

So the complete class number is

510.24 + 62 = 510.246 2

(62 is the number for Engineers in Table 7)

In such cases, it is essential to differentiate between a subject by a specific group of persons and for a specific group of users.

In Area Table,–176 denotes regions where specific religions predominate. Here 176 has been further divided on the basis of some enumerated religions, while all the other unenumerated religions have been placed at 1762–1769, and we are asked to divide 176 by the number following 29 in 292–299 from Table 7.

For example take "Islamic regions of the World". As per above instructions, we will add to the base 176 the number following 29 in 292–299 in Table 7, where number for Islam is 2971. Thus the desired notation for the above area is :

---

* The reader may be again reminded here that by bringing together all the disciplines under the subject of ethics, Dewey has inverted his original pattern of division, viz, division of a discipline by subject. In the 20th edition, (1989) this aberration was withdrawn.

176 + 71 = –17671

Similarly countries where Buddhism prevails is

176 + 43 = –17643

If say our title is "Libraries in Islamic countries of the world", we will proceed as follows:

General Libraries = 027

For geographical treatment, we are to add 027.0 (as the base) the area notation for the specified region from Table 2. Number for Islamic regions as already worked out is 17671. So, the appropriate class number is:

027.0 + 17671= 027.017 671

Wages in Islamic Countries

331.29 + 17671 = 331.291 767 1

Political situation in Buddhist Countries

320.9 + 17643 = 320.917 643

Since all the subdivisions of notation 1 in the Area Table 2 can be added to all the subdivisions 3–9 in the Area Table through the facet indicator 009, so the Table 7 is thus admissible in virtually the whole of the Area table. For example "Islamic Countries of Europe" will be

4 + 009 + 7671= –40097671

(Here note that 1 in 17671 has been removed)

Similarly:

Buddhist Countries of Asia is

5 + 009 + 7643 = –50097643

Therefore:

Libraries in Islamic Countries of Europe is:

027.0 + 40097671 = 027.040 097 671

Political Conditions in Buddhist Countries of Asia

320.9 + 50097643 = 320.950 097 643

The use of Table 7 also occurs through Table 3A, which itself depends on the use of Table 3. In the Table 3A, 352 is specific kind of persons, as subject/theme of literature. As per instructions under –352 (in Table 3A) it is to be further sub-divided by the notation 03–99 from Table 7. For example:

Treatment of lawyers in literature

352 (T3A) + 344 (T7) = –352344

Similarly:

Treatment of Police officials in literature

352 + 3632 = –3523632

Portrayals of Grandparents in literature

352 + 0432 = –3520432

To transform the above numbers in complete examples:

Collection of English Poetry about Lawyers.

82 + 10080 + Notation from Table 3A

= 82 + 10080 + 352344 = 821.008 035 234 4

Treatment of Police Officials in English Drama

82 + 200 + 80 + 352 363 2 = 822.008 035 236 32

Portrayal of Grandparents in English literature

82 + 08 + 0 + 352 043 2

= 820.803 520 432

Another use of Table 7 in Table 3A also occurs at 92 Literature "for and by persons of specific classes". As per instructions, at 392 in 3A, we are to "Add 'persons' notation 04–79 from Table 7 to 92". The reader may be again reminded here that the use of Table 3A is dependent upon the Table 3 itself. Let our title be "Collection of recent Urdu Poetry by Mathematicians".

Urdu Literature	891.439
Poetry	1
Modern Period	7
(7 being taken from the chronological Table)	
Collections (ss Table 3)	08
By specific kinds of persons (Table 3A)	92
By Mathematician from Table 7	51
	891.439 + 1+ 7 + 08 + 92 + 51

891.43917089251 = 891.439 170 892 51

Similarly:

Critical appraisal of Hindi Poetry composed by Blind poets (no period)

891.43 + 1009 (T3) + 92 (T3A) + 08161 (T7)

= 891.431 009 9208161

Critical appraisal of late 20th Century Hindi Drama written by Muslim Dramatists

891.43 + 2 + 7 + 09 + 92 + 2971

= 891.432 709 922971

(Here

2	Drama from Table 3
7	Is period for another special period Table (page 1422)
09	Critical appraisal from Table 3
92	Literature special kind of person from Table 3A
2971	Muslims from Table 7.)

Similarly, in Table 3A, 929 persons occupied with geography history and related disciplines is also divisible by notation 9 from Table 7.

It is, in fact, a corollary of the division in 92 by Table 7.

Collection of recent Urdu Poetry composed by Archaeologists

891.439 + 1 + 7 + 08 + 92 + 93 = 891.439 170 892 93

Collection of English Poetry composed by Professional Historians (No specific period)

821.0080 + 92 (T3A) + 97 (T7) = 821.008 092 97

Collection of recent Urdu Poetry by Historians

891.4391+ 7 + 08 + 92 + 97 = 891.439 170 892 97

Even, if there are no instructions to use the Table 7 at a given situation, and for an extensive class number its use is necessarily required in such situations, the Table 7 can be used through the ss 088.

Historical Paintings drawn by School Children

756 + 088 (Table 1) + 0544 (Table 7) = 756.088 054 4

Paintings of flowers by crippled persons

758.42 + 088 + 08166 = 758.420 880 816 6

Circulation Services to Blinds in Libraries

025.6 + 088 + 08161= 025.608 808 161

Reference Service to Blind People in College Libraries

025.527 + 77 (from 027.7 of Schedules) + 088 + 08161
= 025.527 770 880 816 1

Cookery by School Children

641.5 + 088 + 0544 = 641.508 805 44

Eating Customs of Children

394.12 + 088 + 054 = 394.120 880 54

Reading Habits of Retired Persons

028.9 + 088 + 0696 (T7) = 028.90880696

13

USE OF THE RELATIVE INDEX

The Relative Index has always been an integral part of the DDC system. The Index is called relative as it reverses the pattern of collocation of subjects. In the schedules the first division of the knowledge is by broader disciplines, hence subjects are scattered by discipline. In the index all aspects of a subject dispersed by discipline in the schedules have been converged under one entry. Thus one can see at a glance the different aspects and ramifications of a subject. It is relative as it also depicts the relation of one aspect of a subject to another.

Use of the Index

It is an alphabetical index to every key term occurring in the schedules and all the tables. In addition to the explicit terms, some terms/concepts implied or obtainable through number building process, and popular synonymous terms have also been included. Similarly in the 19th edition index the total number of more than 80,000 entries is far more than the total of 29,528 enumerated entries in the Schedules and Tables combined.

Terms not included

(1) Terms not listed in the Schedules or Tables, i.e., names of all places, minerals, plants, diseases, and so on.
(2) Persons, except for: heads of state who are used to identify historical periods, e.g., Louis XIV; founders of religions, e.g., Muhammad; initiators of schools of thought and discoverers of scientific principles, whose names are usually given in adjectival form, e.g., Darwinian theory.

(3) Names of art or literary forms for particular languages and countries, e.g., American short stories, English poetry, Russian drama, Italian architecture, French cooking.

(4) General concepts that occur in most fields and that are represented by standard subdivisions, e.g., educational administration, language laboratories, mathematical tables, agricultural research, business education.

(5) Concepts that recur in certain contexts may appear to be excluded, but they are normally found under the term for the concept rather than under the term for the context, e.g., World War 2 atrocities, organic acids, radio antennas, television programmes, citizen participation in crime prevention.

Structure

Proper names have been indexed under their AACR-2 form. To use the index, determine the name of the subject of the work in hand. Locate the term used for the subject in its alphabetical position. Under each term will be found listed alphabetically the name of the field of study in which the term is used and the DDC number for the term in that field. When the term is treated in three or more fields of study in the work in hand, the number opposite the heading is to be used; it is the *inter-disciplinary number.*

The arrangement is word by word; and entered as first word capital;

Abra, Philippines
Abrading tools
Asia Minor
Asian
New York
Newark

Phrases have been entered in "Adjective + Noun" form without any inversion as a matter of rule:

Agricultural banks
Colour-television
F-region iconosphere
Fabian socialism
Facial bones
Festive music
Indian Desert
Indian hemp
Indian Ocean

Inorganic chemistry
Paperback books
Reinforced concrete,

Some exceptions to this rule are there: Roman Catholic Bishops has been entered as:

Bishops, Roman Catholic

Compound (hyphenated) words have been treated as if they were a single word. i.e hyphen is ignored.

Franco-German war history
Franconia Ger.
Franconian
Highboys
High-calorie Cookery
High-carbohydrate
High compression-ignition
High-energy
Higher
High-explosive ammunition
Pruning plants crop production
Pruning-equipment, agriculture
Prunings, silviculture

Concrete nouns have been entered in plural form:

Eyeballs
Eye-bar-chain-suspension bridges
Eye-ear-nose-throat diseases
Eyeglasses
Eyelids
Eyes

Abstract nouns have been used in singular form:

man, truth, pathology, system

Modified vowels have been treated as if they were not modified:

Oöita Japan
Oölites

Under each heading entered with first initial letter in capital, all the other aspects or the subjects in which it occurs are listed alphabetically and in subordinated entries the initial letter is not capital, except in case of proper nouns:

Umpiring

American football	796.332 3
baseball	796.357 3
Canadian football	796.335 3

cricket 796.358 3
rugby 796.333 3
soccer 796.334 3
s.a. other spec. games

Structure: of the Index page

Each page of the Relative Index has been divided into two columns by a vertical line in the centre. Each column consists of entries. An entry of the Relative Index is defined as "A term or phrase followed by information in the form either of a number or of a reference to another term or phrase:

Architecture 720
Assam India area -541 62
Or
Boars *see* Sueformes

The index is highly structured both semantically and typographically. Maximum use of indentions and typographical devices has been made to depict rank-relations, and to show different aspects of the concept indexed. Occasionally (in the 19th edition) one has to pass through a maze of referrals to arrive at the apt class number. Cross references conserve space and yet provide a maximum amount of information. A cross reference has been defined as "An instruction note leading from the point at which comprehensive works on a subject are classed (whether stated or implied) to subdivisions of the topic located in numbers other than those subordinate to the number used for comprehensive works." Broadly speaking "see" type cross references are from term/form/spellings not used to those used:

Apes *see* Pongidae
Higher criticism *see* Literary criticism
Tswana *see* Bantu
Zoroastrian music *see* Zoroastrian sacred music
ADP *see* Automatic data processing
UN *see* United Nations

Many a time "see" note refers to remaining aspects of the topic through the phrase "other aspects":

Expectorants pharmcodynamics 615.72
other aspects *see* drugs

Exodus
Bible 222.12
other aspects *see* Historical books (O.T.)

It means that apart from Bible aspect of the Exodus the readers are instructed to see under Historical books (O.T.) for other aspects of Exodus.

In the 19th edition the most important of the cross references is *see also* type, transcribed in abbreviations in the schedules as s.a. This mostly refers to the aspects not covered under the main heading:

Habits	
Child rearing home econ	649.6
Customs *see* social customs	
Psychology	152.33
animals	156.233
children	155.412
s.a. psych of other spec. groups	
s.a. Behaviour	

It means that some related material on habits may be found under the term Behaviour. So we must explore the term Behaviour. Also an *"s.a."* instruction appears under psychology, which in turn appears under Habits. It means that two aspects of habit psychology namely children and animals have been given. For other aspects of habit psychology we are directed to see also psychology of other specific groups. Similarly:

Physiology	
Cells	574.876
animals	591.876
plants	581.876
s.a. specific organism	

It means for Cell physiology of specific organism we are to look under that specific organism. Thus it gives a blanket direction instead of naming every kind of living organism. It is mostly analogous to "Add to..." instructions in the schedules. It conserves enormous space.

Some notes, entries and cross references make full use of abbreviations for recurring concepts. Too frequent use of abbreviations may though retard the efficiency of the beginners, yet it allows two columns a page; and also saves the index and the printed pages from looking too crammed. If the term belongs to any of the seven tables, it is also indicated so through abbreviations. Also the US states when they occur after the name of the city/town are abbreviated. A key to all the abbreviations used in the index has been given preceding the actual index in Volume 3:

Lower
.....
.....
classes *pers* 062 4-062 5
soc. theology
Christianity 261.834 56
comp. rel. 291.178 345 6
s.a. other spec. rel
sociology 305.56

Here the terms/phrases"social theology"; "comparative religion", and see also other specific religions" have been abbreviated.

Under each entry the coordinate and subordinate relations have been shown by indentions. This is rather a very fine and effacious device. Understanding of these indentions is very essential to technical reading of the index. Take an entry Ecology (page 331 of the index, 19th edition):

Ecology
elementary ed. 372.357
life sci 574.5
animals 591.5
man 573
micro organism 576.15
plants 581.5
s.a. spec organism
soc. theology
Christianity 261.836 2
Comp. rel 291.178 362
s.a. other spec. rel
sociology 304.2

To interpret the above: The topic ecology has four main aspects namely: elementary education, life sciences, social theology and sociology. These four aspects are of equal rank among themselves, i.e. form an array. Their equality in rank has been shown typographically as these begin from the same line under the word ecology. Of these life sciences and social theology have some sub aspects. Life sciences has four sub aspects further subarranged alphabetically and one 's.a." note given at the end of this sub entry. Since there is no number against the main term "Ecology" it means there is no interdisciplinary number for ecology; 's.a.' means that for Ecology of specific plants and animals look under that entity. That is for "Ecology of Fishes" one has to look under "Fishes".

Similarly some entry may have sub-sub aspects. For example:

Economic
    assistance
        Internat. politics 327.111
            spec. countries. 327.3-.9

In the above entry Economic assistance has one aspect: international politics, which in turn has another subordinate aspect: specific countries.

At best the foregoing description of the Relative Index is an over simplification of a complex but finely woven pattern. To an uninitiated it may look like a jumbled mass of entries. But soon one learns to follow the structure and locate the desired information.

Need and Importance

Primarily the Relative Index helps those not familiar with the structure of knowledge as in the DDC, thus not familiar with the logical place of a topic in the DDC Schedules.

14

SOME EXAMPLES ILLUSTRATING MULTIPLE SYNTHESIS

Liver Diseases

616.362

Microbiology of Liver Diseases

616.362 + 01 = 616.362 01

Bacterial Diseases of Liver

616.362 + 01 + 4 = 616.362 014

(Added to 01 the number following

616.01 in 616.014 –616.019

The Number for Bacteria is 014

Hence "4" has been added)

Similarly:

Spirochaetalls of Liver Diseases in Human beings (These are kinds of Bacterial Diseases of Liver).

Bacterial Diseases of Liver is:

616.362 + 014

To the base of 616.014 we are to add the number following 589.9 in 589.92–589.99 where spiroachetalls is 589.99. we are to add "9" only

616.362 + 01 + 4 + 9 = 616.362 014 9

Domestic Dogs

636.7

Veterinary Medicine of Domestic Dogs

It will fall under Ceneral principles

636.701–636.708

As per instructions here, we are to add to the base 636.70 (Note the base) the number following 636.0 in 636.01—636.08 where

Veterinary Medicine is 636.089. As per instructions, we will add to 636.70, the number following 636.0 which is "89" here.

Hence, the number is:

636.70 + 89 = 636.708 9

Dog Anatomy

Anatomy is a subject of Veterinary Medicine, so we will first reach the above number as above.

636.7089

To arrive at the number for Dog Anatomy, we will add to 636.089 the number following 61 in 610–619: where Anatomy is 611, thus we will add "1"

Dog Anatomy is

636.7089 + 1 = 636.708 91

Dog Lungs

636.7089 + 124 (from 611.24) = 636.708 912 4

Encyclopaedia of Dog Anatomy

636.7089 + 1003 = 636.708 910 03

Note that class number for Encyclopaedia of Anatomy is 611.003

Tissue Biology of Dogs

636.7089 + 10189 (from 611.0189) = 636.708 910 189

Anatomy of the Tooth Tissue of Dogs

First we will build the class number for the Anatomy of Dog Tissues

636.7089 + 10189 = 636.708 910 189

There at 611.0819, to build the class number for the tooth tissues we have to add to 611.0189 the number for tooth to be taken from 611.1–611.9 where the number for tooth is 611.314 Thus the class number for tooth tissue is

611.0189 + 314 = 611.018 931 4

Anatomy for Tooth Tissues of Dogs is

636.708910189 + 314 = 636.708 910 189 314

Blood Cancer in Dogs

Dogs Animal husbandry 636.7

General Principles of the Animal Husbandry of Dogs have been placed at 636.701 – .708

Veterinary Medicine of Dogs

636.70 + 89 = 636.708 9

For specific aspects of Medicine, we are to add to 089, the number following 61 in 610–619 where blood cancer is 616.99418. Hence, we will add the number following 61, viz. 699418 to the above number.

Hence.

636.7089 + 699418 = 636.708 969 941 8

But if it is Bone Cancer of Dogs, we will have to synthesise 616.994 by the appropriate division of 611 where Bone is 611.71

Hence the complete class number is

636.7089 + 6994 + 71 = 636.708 969 947 1

The following chart will illustrate further:

Animal Husbandry 636	Animal Husbandry of Horses 636.1	Animal Husban–dry of Dogs 636.7
Veterinary Medicine 636.089	Veterinary Medicine of Horses 636.10 + 89 = 636.108 9	Veterinary Medi–cine of Dogs 636.70 + 89 = 636.708 9
Veterinary Anatomy 636.089 + 1 = 636.089 1	(Veterinary) Anatomy of Horses 636.1089 + 1 = 636.108 91	Veterinary Anatomy of Dogs 636.7089 + 1 = 636.708 91
Veterinary Anatomy of Lungs 636.089 + 124 (from 611.24) = 636.089 124	Anatomy of Horse Lungs 636.1 + 089 + 124 = 636.108 912 4	Anatomy of Dog Lungs 636.7 + 089 + 124 = 636.708 912 4

Similarly:

Lung Cancer in Horses

636.1 + 0 + 89 + 6994 + 24 = 636.108 969 942 4

Intestine Cancer in Cattle

636.2 + 0 + 89 + 6994 + 34 = 636.208 969 943 4

Tuberculosis in Cattle

636.2 + 0 + 89 + 6995 = 636.208 969 95

Bone Tuberculosis in Cattle

636.2 + 0 + 89 + 6995 + 71 = 636.208 969 957 1

X–ray Diagnosis of Lung Tuberculosis of Horses

636.1 + 0 + 89 + 6995 + 24 + 07 + 572

= 636.108 969 952 407 572

It is explained as below :

636.1	Animal husbandry of Horses
0	Facet indicator

89	Veterinary Medicine
6995	The number following 61 in 610–619 where number for TB is 616.995
24	Lungs : under 616–995 there is instruction to add to base 616.994, the number following 611 in 611.2 – 611.9, where class number for lungs is 611.24
07	Diagnosis; added as instructed under 616.995 in addition to its extension by the division of 611.
572	X–ray diagnosis; we are asked to add to 07 the number following 616.07 in 616.071–616.079 where 616.075 72 is X–ray diagnosis

Some more examples of Synthesis

Guides to Christian life of Specific Denominations and sects

248.48

For specific sets, we are to add to the above base the number following 28 in 280.2–289.9, e.g.,

Guides to Puritan Life

248.48 + 59 = 248.485 9

If these guides are for specific persons : then to the above add a zero, and to the result the digits following 248.8 in 248.82 – 248.89, say

Guides to Puritan Life for Children

248.4859 + 0 + 2 = 248.485 902

(Number for Children is 248.82)

Similarly

Guides for Methodists

248.48 + 7 = 248.487

Guides for Methodist Children

248.487 + 0 + 2 = 248.487 02

Guides for Methodist divorced men

248.48 + 7 + 0 + 42 + Number following 065 in 0652–0659 from Table 7; where number for divorced men is 0653.

Hence we will add "3"

248.48 + 7 + 0 + 42 + 3 = 248.487 042 3

Administration of a Science Library

Administration of Specific type of Libraries 025.19

(Here, we have been instructed to add to the above base the number following 02 in 026–027, and the number for Libraries devoted to

specific subjects is 026. Hence we will add "6"	6
Again 026 is further to be subdivided like 001–999, and the number for science is 500	5
Hence the class number is :	025.196 5

Similarly

Administration of Libraries on Indian History

025.19 + 6 + 954 = 025.196 954

Administration of Public Libraries in India

025.19 + 74 (from 027.4) + 54 (T2) = 025.197 454

Death Statistics due to Specific Diseases : 312.261–.269

We are asked to add to the base 312.26 the number following 616 in 616.1–616.9. For example, Death due toTuberculosis

312.26 + 995 (from 616.995) = 312.269 95

Death Statistics due to Lung Tuberculosis

Death Statistics due to Tuberculosis (as above)

312.269 95

But the Tuberculosis can further be subdivided as 611, where Lungs is 611.24

Hence the complete class number is

312.26 + 995 + 24 = 312.269 952 4

Rajya Sabha (Upper House of the Indian Parliament)

Legislative bodies have been placed at 328, which is to be subdivided by area :

328.54 Indian Parliament.

Now, as per instructions under 328.4–.9, we are to add the special subdivision enumerated under there; Houses of Parliament fall under the subdivision 07, which is further to be subdivided like 328.31–328.35, the class number for Upper House is 328.31. Hence, we will add 1 to 07, and then 71 to 328.54, to get the complete class number :

328 + 54 (T2) + 07 + 1 = 328.540 71

Similarly:

Financial Powers of the U.S. Senate

328.73 + 07 + 412 = 328.730 741 2

Again

331.124	Job Vacancies (Labour Economics)
331.1242–.1249	Job Vacancies in Technological, Agricultural etc. Occupations.

We are required to add to 331.124 the number following 6 in 620–690.

Let us take:

Job Opportunities in Agriculture

331.124 + 30 = 331.124 3

(The class number for Agriculture is 630)

Similarly:

Job Opportunities in Cotton Agriculture

331.124 + 3351 = 331.124 335 1

(Agriculture of Cotton is 633.51 and we have added to the designated base the number following 6 in 633.51 viz 3351).

Job Opportunities in Cotton Storing

Since 633.51 is further extendable by 631.5 and the class number for Cotton Storing is

633.51 + 68 = 633.516 8

Hence the complete class number for "Job Opportunities in Cotton Storing" is :

331.124 + 3351 + 68 = 331.124 335 168

International Law for Trade in Specific Commodities 341.7547

For individualizing specific commodities, we are required to add to the base 341.7547 the number following 380.14 in 380.141–380.145

For Trade in Agricultural Commodities we have 380.141: so we will add "1" viz, the digits following 380.14 to 341.7547:

341.7547 + 1 = 341.754 71

Not only this, the various Agricultural products can further be individualised by the digits following 63 in 633–638.

International Law of Trade in Wheat

341.7547 + 1 + 311 = 341.754 713 11

(As the class number for wheat is 633.11 and we have added the digits following 63 in 633–638)

Similarly:

International Law of Trade in Coffee

341.7547 + 1 + 373 (from 633.73) = 341.754 713 73

(The class number for Coffee is 633.73)

International Law of Trade in Horses

341.7547 + 1 + 61 = 341.754 716 1

(The class number for Horses is 636.1)

Ministry of Public Health of the Government of India.

354.54 + 06 + 77 = 354.540 677

(To the special subdivision, we have been asked to add the

appropriate digits from 351.01–351.08; since the Department of Public Health is not covered by 351.01–351.06 so it falls in 351.07–.08, where we have been further asked to add from 351.7–351.8, where the number for Public Health Department is 351.77).

Similarly:

Ministry of Labour of the Indian Government
354.54 + 06 + 83 (from 351.83) = 354.540 683

International Law of Trade in Products of Mineral Industries
341.7547 + 2 = 341.754 72

Various mineral products can be specified by adding to the above base the number following 553 in 553.2 – 553.9

International Law for Trade in Marbles
341.7547 + 2 + 512 = 341.754 725 12
(The number for Marbles is 553.512)

International Law for Trade in Diamonds
341.7547 + 2 + 82 = 341.754 728 2
(Class number for Diamonds is 553.82)

Local Administration of Public Telephones
352.91 + 4 (from 351.872–351.878) + 6
(from 384.1–384.6) = 352.914 6

Local Administration of Television
352.91 + 4 + 55 = 352.914 55.

Ministry of Home Affairs of Republic of India

Central Government of various Countries except U.S.A.	354
(For specific countries we have been asked to add the area number for the country concerned to the base 354). Area Number for India (Table 2)	54
To the result, we have been further asked to add special subdivision as given under 354.3–.9). For specific executive departments and Ministries of Cabinet rank	06
under 06 we are further asked to add the digits following 351.0 in 351.01–351.08) Number for Home Ministry is 351.03	3
	= 354.540 63

Similarly:

Ministry of Law and Justice of the

Government of India
354.540 65
Plant Biophysics
Biophysics and Biochemistry
of plants 581.19

Here, we have been asked to divide like 574.191– 574.192, where number for Biophysics is 574.191. Hence the class number for Plant Biophysics is 581.191.

Extraterrestrial Biophysics of Plants
581.19 + 19 = 581.191 9

Here we have added to the base 581.19 the number following 574.19 in 574.191 – 574.192, and the number of Extraterrestrial Biophysics is 574.1919.

Similarly:

Effect of Heat and High Temperature on Plants in Extraterrestrial Space
581.1919 + 62 = 581.191 962.

Biophysics and Biochemistry of Spermatophyta
582.0 + 19 = 582.019

As per instructions, we have added to the base 582.0 the digits following 581 in 581.1–581.19, and the number for Biophysics and Biochemistry therein is 581.19.

As we know that 581.19 is further divisible like 574.191– 574.192, so we can also extend 582.019 further if necessary. For example :

Biophysics of Spermatophyta
582.019 + 1 = 582.019 1

as the number for Biophysics is 574.191

Similarly:

Effect of Cosmic Rays on Spermatophyta
582.019 + 157 = 582.019 157

Effect of Heat and High Temperature on Spermatophyta
582.019 + 162 = 582.019 162

Now let us take a specific kind of Spermatophyta
Trees 582.16

Biophysics and Biochemistry of Trees
582.160 + 19 = 582.160 19

(As per instructions, we have added to the base number 582.160 the digits following 581 in 581.1– 581.8, where the number for Biophysics and Biochemistry is 581.19

This synthesis can further be carried out as before

Biophysics of Trees

582.160 + 191 = 582.160 191

Effect of Heat and High Temperature on Trees

582.160 + 19 + 162 = 582.160 191 62

Genetics of Mollusca

594.0 + 15 = 594.015

(We have added to the base 594.0 the digits following 591 in 591.1 + 591.8, where the number for Genetics is 591.15. The latter is further divisible)

Genetical variations in Mollusca

594.0 + 15 + 8 = 594.015 8

Radiogenetics of Mollusca

594.0 + 15 + 92 = 594.015 92

That is also true of any specified Mollusca

Genetics of Gastropoda

594.3 Gastropoda

As per instruction in the footnote, we add 04 first and then the digits following 591 in 591.1–591.8, where Genetics is 591.15.

Hence:

594.3 + 04 + 15 = 594.304 15

Radiogenetics of Gastropoda

594.3 + 04 + 15 + 92 (from 581.1592 Radiogenetics)

= 594.304 159 2

Synthetic Organic Drugs

615.31

We have been asked to add to 615.31 the digits following 547.0 in 547.01 – 547.08 for specific synthetic drugs of organic nature.

For example:

Organometallic Synthetic Drugs

615.31 + 5 = 615.315

(As the number for organometallic compounds is 547.05, and we have added to the base 615.31 the digit following 547.0 viz "5")

This can further be synthesised to arrive at any specific organometallic drug

For example:

Organosodium synthetic drugs.

For Organometallic drugs, we have 615.315, as above, under 547.05, we see that to obtain a class number for any specified organometallic compound, we have to add to 547.05 the digits following

546 in 546.38–546.68, the number for sodium in the above span is 546.382, so we will add "382" to the above worked out number.

615.315 + 382 = 615.315 382

Similarly:

Organo–nickel Synthetic Drugs

615.31 + 5 + 625 = 615.315 625

(As the class number for Nickel is 546.625)

Organo–Zinc Synthetic drugs

615.31 + 5 + 661 = 615.315 661

(The class number for Zinc is 546.661)

Electrotherapy for Heart Diseases.

For Heart Diseases, we have

616.12

Asterisk here leads us to the special subdivisions under 616.1–616.9 (on pages 868–869)

As per instructions, for therapy, we add "06",

Thus for Heart Therapies we have

616.12 + 06 = 616.120 6

But for specific therapies we have to add to "06" the digits following 615.8 in 615.82–615.89. Since the number for Electrotherapy is 615.845, so we will add "45" to the above.

616.12 + 06 + 45 = 616.120 645 is the complete number.

Similarly :

Electrotherapy for Blood Diseases

616.15 + 06 + 45 = 616.150 645

X–ray therapy for Blood Diseases

616.15 + 06 + 422 (From 615.842 2 X–ray Therapy)

= 616.150 642 2

Surgical Pathology for Female Sterility.

For Female Sterility, we have

618.178

As the asterisk, here leads us to 618.1–618.8 where surgical pathology is 07. Hence, the complete class number is:

618.178 + 07 = 618.178 07

The subdivision "07" can further be subdivided like 616.07 if kind of Pathology is specified:

Diagnosis of Female Sterility

618.178 + 07 + 5 = 618.178 075

(We have added to 07, the digits following 616.07 in 616.071–616.079, and the number for diagnosis is 616.075, so we have added "5")

Similarly:

Diagnosis of Diseases of Pregnancy

618.3 + 07 + 5 = 618.307 5

Chemical diagnosis of Pregnancy Diseases

618.3 + 07 + 56 = 618.307 56

Urianalysis to diagnose Pregnancy Diseases

618.3 + 07 + 566 = 618.307 566

Animal Pests of Wheat

Here Agriculture of wheat is 633.11. The asterisk * leads us to the instructions under 633.635 (p. 1041) and we are required to add "9" to the base number 633.11 for injuries and pests etc. For specific kinds of injuries/diseases/pests, we are asked to divide the resulting number, like 632.1–632.9 The number for Animal Pests is 632.6; so we will add "6" to the above. Hence

633.11 + 9 + 6 = 633.119 6

Individual Animal Pests can be specified as instructed under 632.6. Let us say:

Monkeys as wheat Pests

Wheat	633.11
Pests	9 (as under 633–635 p.1041)
Animal Pests	6 (from 6326)

(We have added the digit following 632 in 632.1–632.9 and for Animal Pests, the number is 632.6).

Monkeys 982

(We have added to "6" the digits following 59 in 592–599, where the number for Monkeys is 599.82).

Hence the complete class number is

633.11 + 9 + 6 + 982 = 633.119 698 2

Similarly:

Rats as wheat Pests

633.11 + 9 + 6 + 93233 = 633.119 693 233

(The class number for Rats is 599.3233)

Rats as Rice Pests

633.18 + 9 + 6 + 93233 = 633:189 693 233

Rats as Potato Pests

633.491 + 9 + 6 + 93233 = 633.491 969 323 3

Insect Pests for Grapes

Grapes Growing	634.8
Pests etc. of Grapes	634.82

(We have been asked to add to the base number 634.82 the digits following 632 in 632.1–632.9, where the number for insect Pests is 632.7 So, we will add "7", and the complete class number thus is

634.82 + 7 = 634.827

As per instructions under 632.7 we can individualise the various insect pests:

Say our title is:

Beetles Insect as Grape Pests

Insect Pest of Grapes 634.82 + 7

To the above, we are to add the digits following 595.7 in 595.71–595.79, where the number for Beetles is 595.76, so we will add "6". Hence the complete class number is:

634.82 + 7 + 6 = 634.827 6

Similarly:

Locust Insect Pests of Grapes

634.82 + 7 + 26 = 634.827 26

Bees (Insect) as Oranges Pests

634.31 + 9 + 7 + 99 = 634.319 799

Bees (Insects) as Apple Pests

634.11 + 9 + 7 + 99 = 634.119 799

Applied Physical Chemistry (viz. Application of Physical Chemistry in Chemical Technology).

660.29

For specific aspect of Physical Chemistry, we are to divide the above number as the base like 541.34–541.39. Let our title be

Applied Photochemistry of specific radiations

660.29 + 53 = 660.295 3

(The class number for Photochemistry of specific radiations is 541.353. We have added to the base the digits following 541.3 viz. "53").

Manufacturing Equipment for shooting Reptiles

Manufacture of equipment for Hunting, fishing and shooting has been placed at

688.79

We have been asked to divide this class number like 799.1–799.3, and shooting Reptiles is 799.279.

Hence the complete class number is

688.79 + 279 = 688.792 79

As per instructions, class number for equipment for shooting individual reptiles can be further individualised:

Manufacturing of Equipment for shooting Crocodiles.

For Reptiles, we have 688.79279. We have been asked at 799.279

to add to it the digits following 597.9 in 597.92 – 597.98. So, we will add here "8" as the class number for Crocodiles is 597.98. Hence

688.79 + 279 + 8 = 688.792 798 is the complete class number.

Similarly:

Equipment for Shooting Turtles (Reptiles)

688.79 + 279 + 2 = 688.792 792

(As the class number for Turtles is 597.92)

Manufacture of Equipment for Shooting Ducks (Birds)

688.79 + 248 + 41 = 688.792 484 1

(As the class number for Ducks is 598.41)

Manufacture of equipment for shooting Turkey (Birds)

688.79 + 248 + 619 = 688.792 486 19

This is not any exhaustive list, but only a representative of the nature of multiple synthesis possible in the schedules. Such cases can be enormously multiplied.

15

CLASSIFICATION OF GENERAL STATISTICS, LAW, GEOGRAPHY AND HISTORY

All these subjects have a common feature that here the "area" though taken from Table 2 is a subject division, and usually occurs as an intervening facet instead of being the last one. It means the area notation is usually further extended by some subject division.

General Statistics

Formula for General Statistics of Specific Countries, localities is:

31(Base) + Area (from Table 2).

General Statistics of Asia

31 + 5 (Table 2) = 315

General Statistics of India

31 + 54 = 315.4

General Statistics of Gujarat

31 + 5475 = 315.475

The law 340 has been first divided by its major branches, preceded by the International Law:

341 International Law
342 Constitutional Law etc.
343 Miscellaneous Public Law
344 Social Law
345 Criminal Law
346 Private Law
347 Civil Procedure and Courts
348 Laws Regulations, Cases
349 Municipal Law

Then in the schedule each branch has been divided by the topic, and each topic under every branch begins with a zero:

344.01 Labour Law

344.02 Social Insurance Law

and so on.

But the preferred arrangement in the DDC is as follows.

The branch is first divided by the country and then by the topic of law:

34X + Area Table + OX

is the citation order:

(Where first X stands for the branch of the law, and the second X for the subtopic of the corresponding branch).

Let us say:

Labour Law in India: Labour Law is a topic of Social Law 344, and the labour law is 344.01. But as per the above citation order, we have

344 + 54 (T2) + 01 (Topic, Labour Law)

= 344.540 1

Obviously this citation order helps to bring together by country all the subtopics of a Branch of Law:

Similarly:

Law of Public Health in India

344 + 54 + 04 = 344.540 4

US Law of Public Health

344 + 73 + 04 = 344.730 4

Library Legislation in Punjab

344 + 54552 + 092 = 344.545 520 92

Supreme Court of India

347 + 54 + 035 = 347.540 35

As per instructions, this can further be subdivided by some special subdivisions enumerated under 347.01 – 347.04

Judges of the Supreme Court of India.

347.54035 + 34 = 347.540 353 4

(34 is for Judges as given under 347.02–347.04)

Law of Evidence in India

347 + 54 + 06 = 347.540 6

Indian Marriage Law

346 + 54 + 016 = 346.540 16

Marriage Law of Texas (USA)

346 + 764 + 016 = 346.764 016

There are also some other topics where subject subdivisions are added after the area. Take for example:

338.93–.99 Economic Development Programmes and policies of specific jurisdictions and group of jurisdiction.

Economic Policies of U.S.A.

338.973

Economic subsidies in U.S.A.

338.973 02

(We have added to the base 338.973, a zero and the digits following 338.92 in 338.922–338.924 where 338.922 is .Subsidies).

Similarly:

Nationalization of Industry in India

338.9 + 54 (Table 2) + 0 + 4 (from 338.924)
= 338.954 04

Communist Parties in India

324.2 + 54 (Table 2) + 075 (Subdivision under 324.24 –.29) = 324.254 075

Conservative Political Parties in Pakistan

324.2 + 5491 (T2) + 04 (as under 324.24 –.29)
= 324.254 910 4

Rules and Procedure of US Senate

328.73 + 05 = 328.730 5

Debates in British Parliament

328 + 41 (Table 2) + 02 (page 239)
= 328.410 2

Management of Youth Hostels in France

647.94 + 44 (Area) + 07 (as under 647.943–647.949)
= 647.944 407

Management of Motels in Canada

647.94+ 71 + 02 = 647.947 102

In case of Geography, the formula is:

91 + Area + Special subdivision (under 914 - 919, page 1443)

Travels in Mughal India

91 + 54 (T2) + 04 (page 1443) + 25 (from 954.025)
= 915.404 25

General Geography of Coastal regions of India

91 + 54 (T2) + 09 (page 1443) + 46 (from 146 of T2)
= 915.409 46

General Geography of Christian dominated areas of India

91 + 54 + 09 + 761 (from 1761 of T2) = 915.409 761

General Geography of Muslim dominated areas of Uttar Pradesh.

91 + 542 + 09 + 76 (from 176 of T2) + 71 (from 2971 of T7) = 915.420 976 71

Travels in Ancient China

91 + 31 + 04 (Special subdivisions under 913.1 –.9) = 913.104

Physical Geography of Ancient Macedonia

91 + 381 + 02 = 913.810 2

Physical Geography of United States

91 + 73 + 02 = 917.302

Travels in Texas

91 + 764 + 04 = 917.640 4

General Geography of Forest Regions of Texas

91 + 764 + 09

(Special subdivision under 914–919)

+ 52 (from 152 in T2) = 917.640 952

General Geography of the Hilly Regions of Greater Punjab of India

91 + 545 + 09 + 43 = 915.450 943

Similarly, the formula for History is:

9 + (Area from Table 2) + Period subdivision from 940–999)

History of India

9 + 54 = 954

India under the reign of Akbar

9 + 54 + 0254 (from 954.0254) = 954.025 4

History of Punjab

9 + 545 (from T2) = 954.5

History of Punjab during the reign of Akbar

9 + 545 (T2) + 0254 (from 954.0254) = 954.502 54

History of Jammu & Kashmir during British Rule

9 + 546 + 03 = 954.603

16

SOME MORE ILLUSTRATED EXAMPLES

(A) Use of Standard Subdivisions

Journal of Public Administration
350.000 5

Journal of Aptitude Tests
153.940 005

Research in Public Administration in UK
350.000 720 41

Research in the Local Governments of UK
352.0 + 41072 = 352.041 072

Research in U.S.A. on the Local Governments of UK
352.0 + 41 (T2) + 072 (T1) + 0 + 73 (T2) = 352.041 072 073

Research in the Central Govt. of India
354 + 54 (T2) + 00072 (T1) = 354.540 007 2

Research in UK in the Central Govt. of India
354 + 54 (T2) + 00072 (T1) + 0 + 41 (T2)
= 354.540 007 204 1

Statistical Principles of Biology
574 + 015 (T1) + 195 (From 519.5) = 574.015 195

Dictionary of Algebra in Spanish
512 + 003 (T1) + 61 (T6) = 512.003 61

Indian Trade Catalogues for Furniture
684.1 + 00294 (T1) + 54 (T2) = 684.100 294 54

Directory of Universities Teaching Journalism in Japan
070 + 0711 (T1) + 52 (T2) = 070.071 152

Journalism in 19th Century
070 + 9034 (T1) = 070.903 4

Journalism in UK in 19th Century
072 + 09034 (T1) = 072.090 34
Journalism in British Colonies in 19th Century
079 + 1712 (T2) + 41 (T2) + 034 (from 09034)
= 079.171 241 034
Journalism in Muslim Countries
079.176 7
Journalism in Muslim Countries in 19th Century
079.176 703 4
Journalism in Portuguese Speaking area of India
079.175 (T2) + 69 (T6) + 0 + 54 (T2)
= 079.175 690 54
Journalism in Canada in 19th Century
071.103 4
Female Journalists
070 + 088 (T1) + 042 (T7) = 070.088 042
Contribution of Pakistanis to Journalism
070 + 089 (T1) + 91412 (T5) = 070.089 914 12
Contribution of Indians to Library Classification
025.4 + 089 (T1) + 91411 (T5) = 025.4089 914 11
Economic Conditions in Muslim dominated Parts of India
330.9 + 176 (T2) + 7 (from 292–299 of schedule) + 0
+ 54 (T2) = 330.917 670 54

Other alternative as described under – 3– 9 in Table 2 (p. 27) is as follows:

330.9 + 54 + 009 + 76 (from Table 2, deleting 1) + 7 (from
292 – 299 from Schedule) = 330.954 009 767
Economic conditions in Christian dominated parts of India
330.917 610 54
Or
330.954 009 761

Here if Time period is required, it is to be taken from the History schedule of that country.

Economic conditions in Christian dominated parts of India during 1971 – 1977

330.917 610 540 51
Or
330.954 009 761 051
Political conditions in Non–aligned Countries of Africa
320.9 + 1716 (T2) + 0 + 6 (T2) = 320.917 160 6
Or

320.9 + 6 (T2) + 009 + 716 (from 1716, T2)
= 320.960 097 16

Political conditions in Non-aligned Countries of Africa during 1970–1979

320.9 + 1716 (T2) + 0 + 6 (T2) + 827 (from 909.827)
= 320.917160682 7

Or

320.960 097 160 327

Social change in Indian Villages

303.4 + 0954 (T1 & 2) + 009 + 734 (T2 deleting 1)
= 303.409 540 097 34

Social change in Hindi Speaking area of India

303.4 + 0954 (T1 & 2) + 009 + 75 (T2 deleting 1)
+ 9143 (T6) = 303.409 540 097 591 43

History of the Third World

909.09 + 724 (from T2, following 1) = 909.097 24

History of the Third World during 1990-1999

909.09 + 724 (from 1724, T1) + 0 + 829 (From 909.829)
= 909.09724 + 0 + 829 = 909.097 240 829

World History of the Communist Bloc

909.09 + 717 (from 1717, T2) = 909.097 17

History of Christian Nations since 19th Century

909.09 + 761 (from 1761, T2) + 08 (from 909.8)
= 909.097 610 8

History of English Speaking nations

909.09 + 75 (from 175, T2) + 21 (T6) =
909.09 + 75 + 21 = 909.097 521

(B) Titles Requiring the addition of two areas from Table 2

Migration of people from India to U.S.A

304.8 + 73 + 0 + 54 = 304.873 054

Please note that the country towards which migration occurs is to be taken first and the place of origin comes later.

Migration to U.S.A. from Poor Countries

304.8 + 73 + 0 + 1724 = 304.873 017 24

Migration to U.S.A. from Poor Countries during 1990-1999

304.87301724 + 048 (from 09048, T1) = 304.873 017 240 48

Migration of Buddhists to Europe

304.8 + 4 + 0 + 176 + 43 (from 292–299) = 304.840 176 43

Exchange Rate between US dollar and Indian Rupee

332.45609 + 73 + 0 + 54 = 332.456 097 305 4

Conversion of Euro into Pound Sterling

332.45609 + 4 (T2) + 0 + 41 (T2) = 332.456 094 041

Tables and Formulas for Conversion of Euro into other currencies

332.45609 + 4 (T2) + 00212 (T1)
= 332.456 094 002 12

British Colonies in Asia

325.3 + 41+ 09 + 5 = 325.341 095

British Colonies in Indian Ocean Area

325.3 + 41 + 09 + 165 = 325.341 091 65

Artists in Muslim regions of India

709.54009 + 76 (Table 2 without digit 1) + 7 (from 297 of Table 7)
= 709.540 097 67

Muslim Artists

704 + 297 (T7) = 704.297

British financial investment in the Third World

332.673 + 41 + 0 + 1724 = 332.673 410 172 4

US foreign investment in Pakistan

332.673 + 73 (T2) + 0 + 5491 (T2) = 332.673 730 549 1

Foreign Investment of French Community in Muslim Countries

332.673 + 1712 (T1) + 44 (T2) + 0 + 176 (T1)
+ 71 (2971 (T7)) = 332.673 171 201 767 1
= 332.673 171 244 017 671

Emigration from India to U.S.A.

325.2 + 54 + 0 + 73 = 325.254 073

(Here the country entered comes later in the citation order, and the country of departure comes first).

Emigration from India to English Speaking Countries.

325.254 017 521

Emigration from India to English Speaking Countries of Europe

325.254 017 521 04

Foreign relations between U.S.A. and Muslim countries

327.73 (T2) + 0 + 176 (T1) + 71 (from 2971 (T7))
= 327.73017671

Foreign relations of Israel with Muslim Countries

327.569 401 7671

Foreign relations of Israel with Muslim Countries of Asia
327.5694 + 0 + 176 (T1) + 71 (from 2971 (T7)
+ 05 (Asia as under — 1 T1 (p. 14, Vol. 1)
= 327.569 401 767 105

Foreign relations of India with British Commonwealth Countries
327 + 54 (T2) + 0 + 1712 (T2) + 41 (T2)
327.540 171 241

Foreign relations of British Commonwealth Countries
327.091 712 41

Labour Workers from Nepal in India
331.62 + 5496 + 0 + 54 = 331.625 496 054

Labour workers from Pakistan in Middle East
331.62 + 549 + 0 + 56 = 331.625 490 56

India's economic assistance to Nepal
338.91 + 54 + 0 + 5496 = 338.915 405 496

Economic aid from U.S.A. to developing Countries
338.917 301 724

Economic aid from British Commonwealth countries to Poor Nations
338.911 712 410 172 4

Trade between Japan and Canada
382.09 + 52 + 0 + 71 = 382.095 207 1

Trade between Arab countries and the Third World
382.091 + 174 (T2) + 927 (T5) + 0 + 1724 (T2)
= 382.091 174 927 017 24

Trade agreements between Japan and Canada
382.9 + 52 + 0 + 71 = 382.952 071

Public Libraries in Developing Countries
027.409 172 4

(C) Examples Depicting Synthesis from the Schedules

Administration of University Libraries
025.19 + 77 (from 027.7) = 025.197 7

Administration of Prison Libraries : A manual
025.19 + 7665 (from 027.665) + 0202 (T1)
= 025.197 665 020 2

Document Selection in University Libraries
025.218 + 77 = 025.218 77

Book Selection in Prison Libraries

025.218 + 7665 = 025.218 766 5

Book Selection on International Law

025.27 + 341 = 025.273 41

Book Selection on Collection Development in Libraries

025.27 + 0252 = 025.270 252

Selection and Procurement of Govt. Publications

025.28 + 34 + 025.283 4

Acquisition of Microforms in Libraries

025.28 + 94 = 025.289 4

Microform Acquisitions on International Law in University Libraries

025.27 + 341 = 025.273 41

(We will have to ignore the facets of University and Microforms, as there is no provision to add them. Readers may ask why the document has not been classed in University libraries or in Acquisition of Microforms. We have applied here the Principle of Precedence. According to this principle, unless stated otherwise or given some specific order of precedence, the number coming first in the schedule will have precedence over other facets. In the above title, the class number that comes first is 025.27 Book Selection. This number as per rule can have any of the two facets either of format of the documents or of subject of the document. Since the subject of material comes first in the schedule, hence it will be considered, and the second facet "of Format" will have to be ignored).

Problem of Serial Procurements in Natural Science in Public Libraries

025.27 + 32 = 025.273 2

Jain Religious Calendar

294.4 + 36 = 294.436

Statistics of Deaths due to injuries:

Please note that it is not any specific disease, so will not fall in 312.261–.265. It will fall under 312.2604 where we have been asked to add to the above base the digits following 61 in 617–618. Since the class number for injuries is 617.1, so we add "71". Hence the number is:

312.2604 + 71 = 312.260 471

Statistics of deaths due to complications of Pregnancy

312.2604 + 83 = 312.260 483

(The class number for complication of pregnancy is 618.3)

Job Opportunities in Documentation

331.1241 + 025 (from schedule) = 331.124 102 5

Job Opportunities in Agriculture

331.124 + 30 = 331.124 3

(We have added to the base 331.124, the digits following 6 in 620–690. The class number for Agriculture is 630, you know).

Similarly:

Job mobility among Librarians

331.1291 + 020 = 331.129 102

Job mobility in Agriculture occupation

331.129 + 30 = 331.129 3

Service condition in Agricultural Occupations

331.204 + 30 = 331.204 3

Wages of Documentalists

331.281 + 025 = 331.281 025

Wages in Agricultural occupations

331.28 + 30 = 331.283

Agricultural Workers Union

331.881 + 30 = 331.881 3

(*cf.* professional associations with ss –06)

Labour Management disputes in Documentation Centres

331.89041 + 025 = 331.890 410 25

Labour disputes of Agriculture labour

331.8904 + 30 = 331.890 43

Strikes by Documentalists

331.89281 + 025 = 331.892 810 25

Strikes by Agricultural Workers

331.8928 + 30 = 331.892 83

Cooperation in Documentation Services

334.681 + 025 = 334.861 025

History of Cooperative Agriculture

334.68 + 309 (from 630.9) = 334.683 09

Economics of Poultry Farming

338.17 + 65 (from 633–638,where Poultry is 636.5) = 338.176 5

Economics of Metal Extractions

338.27 + 4 (from 553.2–553.9) = 338.274

Administration of Telephone system by the Govt.

351.874 + 6 (from 384.1–384.6) = 351.874 6

Government Administration of Television

351.874 + 55 (from 384.55) = 351.874 55

Government Administrative of TV in India

354 + 54 (T2) + 00 (as under 001-009 of 354.3-9 p. 444, Vol. 2) + 874 (from 351.874) + 55 (from 384.55)

= 354.540 087 4 55

Foreign Ministry of Kenya

354 + 6762 (T2) + 06

(As instructed under 354.3–.9) + 1 (from 351.01 – 351.08; for foreign ministry we have 351.01) = 354.676 206 1

Ministry of Defence of the Govt. of Canada

354.710 66

Social Welfare Ministry of the Indian Govt.

354.54 + 06 + 84 = 354.540 684

Vice-President of the Republic of India

354.54 + 0 + 318 (from 351.003 18) = 354.540 318

Rashtriya Panchayat (Parliament) of Nepal

328.5496 = 328.549 6

Debates in Rashtriya Panchayat Nepal

328 + 5496 (T2) + 02 (as under 328.4–.9)
= 328.549 602

Social Welfare Services for Cancer Patients.

362.19 + 6994 (from 616 – 618) = 362.196 994

Social Welfare for Patients suffering from Lung Cancer

362.19 + 6994 + 24 (from 611.2 –611.9)
= 362.196 994 24

Social effects of alcoholism

362.292 + 3 (from special sub-divisions under 362–363)
= 362.292 3

Reform movements for Alcoholics

362.292 + 5 (from special sub-divisions under 362–363)
+ 24 (from 361.2–361.8) = 362.292 524

Reform movements for Drug addicts

362.293 + 5 + 24 = 362.293 524

Social Assylums for the Mentally retarded people

362.3 + 85 = 362.385

Providing Shelter to Flood victims

363.3493 + 83 = 363.349 383

Teaching methods for the Deaf Students

371.912 + 3 (from 371.904 2 – 371.9046) = 371.912 3

Teaching equipment for the education of the mentally retarded

371.928 + 0 + 5 (from 371.9042–371.9046) =
371.928 05

Corporal punishment in elementary schools

372.1 + 542 (from 371.1–371.8) = 372.154 2

Teaching through audio-visuals in Elementary schools
372.1 + 335 = 372.133 5

Science Curriculum in Elementary schools
372.35 + 043 (Special sub-divisions under 372.3–372.8) = 372.350 43

Corporal punishment in Secondary Schools
373.1 + 542 (from 371.1–371.8) = 373.154 2

Teaching through audio-visuals in Secondary Schools
373.1 + 335 = 373.133 5

Teaching through audio-visuals in Universities
378.17 + 35 (from 371.3028–371.397 where AVs are 371.335) = 378.173 5

Medical care for the Universities students
378.19 + 712 (from (371.6–371.8) = 378.197 12

Folk Tales about Elephants
398.2452 + 961 (from 592–599, where elephant is 599.61) =398.245 296 1

Rose in Folk tales
398.368 + 3372 (from 582–589 where rose is 583.372) = 398.368 337 2

Satellites of the Planet Saturn
523.98 + 6 (from 523.4–523.48 where Saturn is 523.46) = 523.986

Hindu (Chronological) Calendar
529.32 + 45 (from 292–299 where Hindu religion is 294.5) = 529.324 5

Supersonic Velocity in Aerodynamics
533.62 + 75 (from 533.21–533.29) = 533.627 5

Acceleration of Meson Particles
539.737 + 62 (from 539.7211–539.7217 where Meson is 539.72162) = 539.737 62

Radioactive isotopes Inorganic chemical substances (it is a topic of Inorganic Physical Chemistry)
546.26 + 88 (from 541.34–541.39 where radioactive isotopes is 541.388) = 546.268 8

Radioactive isotopes of Radium
546.396 + 5 (Special subdivision under 546) + 88 (from 541.34—541.39) = 546.396 588

Physical Chemistry of organic chemicals
547.1 + 3 (from 541.2 – 541.7) = 547.13

Radioactive isotopes of organic substances

547.1 + 3884 (from 541.2–517.7) = 547.138 84

Radioactive isotopes of Hydrocarbons

547.01 + 045 (special subdivisions under 547)+884 (from 541.34 –547.39) = 547.010 458 84

Radioactive isotopes of the Hydrocarbons in Aromatic Chemistry

547.61 + 045 + 884 (from 547.34–541.39) = 547.610 458 84

Organic Aromatic acids

547.63 + 7 (from 547.035 – 547.038) = 547.637

Analytical biochemistry of Plants

581.19 + 285 (from 574.191–574.192) = 581.192 85

Biophysics and biochemistry of Spermatophyta

582.0 + 19 (from 581.1–581.3) = 582.019

Biochemistry of Spermatophyta

582.0 + 19 + 2 (from 574.91 –574.192 where biochemistry is 574.192) =582.019 2

Analytical biochemistry of Spermatophyta

582.0 + 19 + 285 (from 574.191–574.192, where analytical biochemistry is 574.19285 = 582.019 285

Similarly:

Biochemistry of organic compounds of spermatophyta plants

582.0 + 19 + 24 = 582.019 24

Each of the organic compounds can be specified as instructed under 574.192 4

Biochemistry of Steroids (organic compounds) in Supermatophyta

582.0 + 19 + 24 + 3 (from 547.72–547.78 where steroids is 547.73) =582.019 243

Biochemistry of glucose in Spermatophyta

582.0 + 19 + 24 + 813 = 582.019 248 13

Animal Biochemistry

591.19 + 2 (from 574.191–574.192) = 591.192

Analytical biochemistry of Animals

591.19 + 285 (Analytical biochemistry is 574.19285) = 591.192 85

Organic compounds in animal biochemistry

591.19 + 24 = 591.192 4

Function of Steroids (organic compounds) in animal biochemistry.

591.19 + 24 + 3 (from 547.72–547.78 where steroids is 547.73) = 591.192 43

Function of glucose in animal biochemistry
591.19 + 24 + 813 (glucose is 547.7813) = 591.192 481 3
Biophysics and Biochemistry of Invertebrates
592.0 + 19 (from 591.1–591.8) = 592.019
Biochemistry of Invertebrates
592.0 + 19 (from 591.1– 591.8)+2 (from 574.191–574.192) = 592.019 2
Biochemistry of organic compounds in Invertebrates
592.0 + 19 + 24 (from 574.191–574.192, where bio–chemistry of organic compounds is 574.1924) = 592.019 24
Biochemistry of Steroids (organic compounds) in Invertebrates
592.0 + 19 + 24 + 3 (from 547.74–547.78, where steroids is 547.73) = 592.019 243
Glucose in the Biochemistry of Insects
595.70 + 19 + 24 + 813 (Glucose is 547.7813 in 547.72–547.78) = 595.701 924 813
Biochemistry of Orthoptera (Insects)
595.726 + 04 (as instructed under 592–599) + 19 (from 591.1–591.8 as instructed under –04) + 2 (as instructed under 591.19) = 595.726 041 92
Analytical biochemistry of Orthoptera (Insects)
595.726 + 04 + 19 + 285 = 595.726 041 928 5
Biochemistry of organic compounds in Orthoptera (Insects)
595.726 + 04 + 19 + 24 = 595.726 041 924
Biochemistry of Steroids (organic compounds) in Orthoptera (Insects)
595.726 + 04 + 19 + 24 + 3 (from 547.72 – 547.78) = 595.726 041 924 3
Biochemistry of glucose in Orthoptera (Insects)
595.726 + 04 + 19 + 24 + 813 = 595.726 041 924 813
Biochemistry of glucose in primates
599.8 + 04 + 19 + 24 + 813 = 599.804 192 481 3
Synthetic Halogenated organic drugs
615.31 + 2 (from 547.01 –547.08 where Halogenated compounds is 547.02) = 615.312
Organometallic Synthetic drugs
615.31 + 5 (from 547.01–547.08 where organometallic compounds is 547.05) = 615.315
Synthetic organoaluminium drugs
615.31 + 5 + 673 (Following 546 in 546.38–546.68,

where aluminium is 546.673) = 615.315 673

Synthetic organo–potassium drugs

615.31 + 5 + 383 (from 546.38–546.68 where Potassium is 546.383) = 615.315 383

Copper Poison

615.925 + 652 (from 546.2–546.7 where copper is 546.652) = 615.925 652

Lead Poison

615.925 + 688 = 615.925 688

Diagnosis of Lungs Diseases

616.24 + 07 (as instructed under 616.1–616.9 where pathology is 07) + 5 (from 616.071 –616.079 where diagnosis is 616.075) = 616.240 75

Electrical diagnosis of Lungs Diseases

616.24 + 07 + 56 = 616.240 756

Spurious Therapies of Small–pox

615.912 Smallpox is an * asterisked class number. At the footnote we have been asked to add special subject divisions as instructed under 616.1–616.9 (pp. 868–869); there therapies is 06. To specify various therapies, we have been asked to add to 06 the digits 'following 615.8 in 615.82–615.89; Spurious therapies is 615.856. Hence,

615.912 + 06 + 56 = 615.912 065 6

Electrotherapy for Diseases of Bones

616.71 + 06 + 45 = 616.710 645

Climatotherapy for Tuberculosis

616.995 + 06 + 34 = 616.995 063 4

Climatotherapy for Tuberculosis of Bones

(Tuberculosis is 616.995 for TB of any organ, we have been asked to divide 616.995 like 611.1 – 611.9, where bone is 611.71. Thus the class number for bone TB is 616.995 + 71 = 616.995 71

The special subject Subdivisions given under 616.1—616.8 are still applicable here. Hence: 616.99571 + 06 + 34 = 616.995 710 634 is the required number

Drug therapy for Pulmonary Tuberculosis

616.995 + 24 + 061 = 616.995 240 61

X–ray diagnosis of Bones Tuberculosis

616.995 + 71 (from 611.1–611. 9) + 07 (special sub–divisions

under 616.1–616.9) + 572 (from 616.071 – 616.079)
= 616.995 710 757 2

Rib Fractures
617.15 + 2 (from 611.711–611.718 where ribs is 611.712) = 617.152

Drug Therapy for Dental Diseases
617.63 + 061 (from special divisions under 617) = 617.630 61

Electro Therapy for diseases of gums
617.632 + 06 + 45 (from 615.82–615.89 where Electrotherapy is 615.845) = 617.632 064 5

Nutritional Diseases in Children
618.92 + 39 (from 616.1–616.9 where Nutritional Diseases is 616.39) = 618.923 9

Case histories in Children Diseases
618.920 + 09 (from special sub-divisions under 616.1–616.9, where case histories is 09) = 618.920 09

Lighting in Museum Buildings
621.322 + 76 (from 725–728 where Museum Buildings is 727.6) = 621.322 76

Lighting in Biological Museum Buildings
621.322 + 76 + 574 (from 001 –999 where Biology is 574) = 621.322 765 74

Lighting in Pottery Museums
621.322 + 76 + 6663 (from 001–999 where Pottery is 666.3) = 621.322 766 663

Lighting in Hospital Libraries
621.322 + 782 (from 725–728 where general libraries is 727.82) + 662 (from 027.1–027.8 where Hospital libraries is 027.662) = 621.322 782 662

Concrete as Foundation material in Civil Engineering
624.153 + 36 (from 620.12–620–19 where concrete is 620.136) = 624.153 36

Repair of Bicycles
629.287 + 72 (from 629.2204 –629.229, where bicycles is 629.2272) = 629.287 72

Chemistry of Agriculture
630.2 + 40 (from 510–590)=630.24

Physical Chemistry of Agriculture
630.2 + 413 (from 510–590 where physical chemistry is 541.3) = 630.241 3

Fertilizers for Fruit Orchards
634.04 + 89 (from special subdivisions under 633–635 as per instructions in the footnote on page 1046) = 634.048 9

Nitrate Fertilizers for Fruit Orchards
634.04 + 89 + 42 (from 631.81–631.87) where Nitrate Fertilizer is 631.842) = 634.048 942

Nitrate Fertilizers for Lemons
634.334 + 89 + 42 = 634.334 894 2

Nitrate Fertilizers for Flower and Ornamental Plants
635.91 + 842 (from 631.2—631.8) = 635.918 42

Poultry Feed
636.50 + 855 (from 636.01–636.08 where Feed is 636.085 5) = 636.508 55

Bee Farming
638.57 + 99 (from 595.71–595.79 where Bee is 595.799) = 638.579 9

Snake Farming
639.39 + 6 (from 597.92–597.98 where snakes is 592.96) = 639.396

Snake Farming in South India
639.396 + 09548 = 639.396 095 48

Food value of Oranges
641.34 + 31 (from 634.1–634.8 where oranges is 634.31) = 641.343 1

Home construction of children clothes
646.40 + 6 (from 646.31–646.36 where children clothing is 646.36) = 646.406

Home construction of raincoats for women
646.453 + 0 + 4 = 646.453 04

Rearing of Children in Royal Families
649.15 + 62 (from 371.91–371.97 where royalty is 371.962) = 649.156 2

Rearing of Deaf Children
649.15 + 12 = 649.151 2

Rearing of Jew Children
649.15 + 7 (from 371.91–371.97 where children of racial,

ethnic and national origin is 371.97) + 924 (from Table 5 for Jews) = 649.157 924

Rearing of Jew children in U.S.A.

649.157924 + 0 + 73 (as per instructions under 371.97) = 649.157 924 073

Rearing of Punjabi children in Canada

649.15 + 7 + 9142 + 0 + 71 = 649.157 914 207 1

Cost accounting in hospitals

657.8322 + 0 + 42 (from 657.1–657.7 where Cost Accounting is 657.42) = 657.832 204 2

Cost Accounting in Government Offices

657.835 + 0 + 42 = 657.835 042

Auditing of hospital accounts

657.8322 + 0 + 45 = 657.832 204 5

Marketing of Rugs and Carpets

658.809 + 7467 (from 001 –999 where Rugs and Carpets is 746.7) = 658.809 746 7

Advertising Rugs and Carpets

659.19 + 7467 = 659.197 467

Industrial production of Nitrogen Compounds

661.0 + 711 (from 546.4–546.7 where Nitrogen is 546.711) = 661.071 1

Industrial thermochemistry

660.29 + 6 (from 541.34–541.39 where Thermochemistry is 541.36) = 660.296

Industrial properties of anthracite coal

662.222 + 5 (from 553.21–553.25 where anthracite coal is 553.25) = 662.222 5

Pasteurization in Industrial production of Wines

663.20 + 5 (from 663.11–663.19 where Pasteurization is 663.15) = 663.205

Pasteurization in Industrial production of Grapewine

663.2204 + 5 = 663.220 45

Journal of Pottery technology

666.3 + 5 (from ss 01–09) = 666.35

Research in Pottery Technology

666.3 + 72 (from ss 072) = 666.372

Research in U.S.A. in Pottery Technology

666.3 + 72 + 0 + 73 (Area) = 666.372 073

All India Conference on Pottery Technology
666.3 + 6 + 0 + 54 = 666.360 54

Industrial Manufacturing of Nitro-dyes
667.25 + 2 (from 547.862–547.867 where Nitro-dyes is 547.862) = 667.252

Industrial Dyeing of Silk
667.3 + 39 (from 677.1–677.5 where Silk is 677.39) = 667.339

Industrial dyeing of polyester Textiles
667.3 + 4743 = 667.347 43

Industrial Production of Urea (Fertilizer)
668.62 + 41 (from 631.83–631.85 where Urea is 631.841) = 668.624 1

Industrial Production of Sodium Nitrate Fertilizer
668.62 + 42 = 668.624 2

Physical Metallurgy of Copper
669.96 + 3 (from 669.1–669.7 where Copper is 669.3) = 669.963

Manufacture of Ultraviolet rays Spectroscopes
681.414 + 4 (from 535.842–535.846 where Ultraviolet light is 535.844) = 681.414 4

Manufacture of Infrared rays Speçtroscopes
681.414 + 2 = 681.414 2

Manufacturing of Guitars
681.81 + 761 (from 786.2 – 789.6 where guitar is 787.61) = 681.817 61

Manufacture of Hockey sticks
688.76 + 355 (from 796.1–796.9 where hockey is 796.355) = 688.763 55

Manufacture of equipment for ice skating
688.76 + 91 = 688.769 1

Installing Air Conditioning in Museums
697.93 + 76 (from 725–728 where Museum Building is 727.6) = 697.937 6

Installation of Air Conditioning in Biological Museums
697.93 + 76 + 574 (from 001–999 where biology is 574) = 697.937 657 4

Installing Air Conditioning in Hospital library buildings
697.93 + 782 (from 725–728 where general libraries is 727.82) + 662 (from 027.1–027.8 where hospital libraries is 027. 662) = 697.937 826 62

Installing Air Conditioning in Residential Buildings
697.93 + 8 = 697.938

Depiction of Buddhistic themes in Art Works
704.9489 + 43 (Following 29 in 292–299, where Buddhism is 294.3) = 704.948 943

Medical Objects as Art works
704.949 + 61 (from 000–999) = 704.949 61

Use of Prefabricated material in Architectural Construction
721.0449 + 7 (from 669.1–669.7 where Prefabricated material is 669.97 = 721.044 97

Use of plastic in Architectural construction
721.0449 + 9 (from 693.99) + 23 (from 620.1923) = 721.044 992 3

Architecture of Buildings for indoor games with special reference to handicapped persons
725.84 + 042 (Special subdivision from 721–729) = 725.840 42

Architecture of Hindu temples
726.1 + 45 (from 292–299 where Hinduism is 294.5) = 726.145

Architecture of Library Science School Buildings
727.4 + 02 (from 001–999) = 727.402
Whereas the Architecture of Library Buildings is placed at 727.8 which is amenable to further expansion

Architecture of General Library Buildings
727.82

Architecture of Hospital Libraries
727.82 + 662 (from 027.662) = 727.826 62

Maintenance and repair of Hospital Libraries
727.82 + 662 + 0289 (page 1238) = 727.826 620 289

Effects of Social Conditions on the Architecture of the National Library of India
727.82 + 5 (from 027.5) + 54 (Area Table) + 010 (page 1238) + 3 (from 700.103) = 727.825 540 103

Architecture of Club Houses keeping in view the special needs of aged people.
728.4 + 042 (from the special subdivisions under 721–729) = 728.404 2

Drawings of Reptiles
743.6 + 79 (from 592–599, where reptiles is 597.9) = 743.679

Drawings of Penguin Birds
743.6 + 8441 (from 592–599 where Penguin is 598.441) = 743.684 41

Paintings depicting Social Life
758.9 + 301 (from 001–999) = 758.930 1

Photography of Animals
778.538 + 590 (from 001–999) = 778.538 59

Bird Photography
778.538 + 598 = 778.538 598

Fishing Sharks
799.17+ 31 (from 597.2–597.5, where Sharks is 597.31) = 799.173 1

Sacred Music of the Sikhs
783.029 + 46 (from 292–299 where Sikhism is 294.6) = 783.029 46

Scores on Jazz Music
785.42 + 5 (from special subdivisions under 785.1–785.8)=785.425

Dewey Decimal Classification for Indians
025.431 + 024 (T1) + 03 (T7) + 91411 (T5) = 025.431 024 039 141 1

17

AN UPDATE: BRIEF INTRODUCTION TO THE 19th (1979), 20th (1989) AND 21st (1996) EDITIONS

1. INTRODUCTION

The DDC, one of the big three classifications is the most popular of all the library classification systems. It is used in 2,00,000 libraries in 135 counties including national bibliographies of 59 countries, and has been translated in over 30 languages. It has secured and retained this position partially because of its well defined revision policy, sound revision machinery and marketing techniques. First revised in 1885, it has constantly and regularly been revised. Revision has been described as a double edged sword which cuts both ways. Though essential for survival too much of it may be killing and dangerous to its popularity and atrocious for its users. So a revision policy has to be carefully formulated, and has to make a delicate balance between change and stability. A new edition incorporates new topics at appropriate places that have emerged since the previous edition, and deletes some of the obsolete subjects. But as an equally important task it relocates some topics to better deemed places in view of changed structure of knowledge. Many subjects are expanded in details. In addition, advantage is taken to apply new classificatory techniques in improving the system. Edition by edition the system is becoming more and more faceted, user friendly, technically and intellectually better.

1.1 Revision procedure

To carry out the revision there is a full time editorial team headed by the (chief) editor of the DDC. The editorial office is located in the Decimal

Classification Division of the Library of Congress, Washington, D.C., USA since 1953. This Division applies DDC numbers to more than one lakh new but select books every year procured in the Library of Congress. There is ten-member Decimal Classification Editorial Policy Committee (DCEPC) headed by a chairperson to advise the editors on the kind and extent of revision. This is a broadbased international committee appointed jointly by the American Library Association (ALA) and the Forest Press, the publisher of the DDC. The Committee has representatives from Canada, the UK, Australia and from every sector of the US library profession. It is an apex committee which minutely advises and oversees the editing including changes and innovations in the system. Its decisions are executed by the chief editor and his/her team of assistant editors who have their office in the Decimal Classification Division of the Library of Congress, Washington, D.C. Its new editions are published at an interval ranging from 7 to 10 years by its exclusive publisher the Forest Press till recently located at Albany, New York. It has now moved its office to OCLC headquarters at Dublin, Ohio. It is headed by an Executive Director, who is a vice-president of the OCLC.

1.2 Communication and incorporation of changes

Revision of the DDC is a continuous process. After deliberations and discussions when the changes or additions are approved by the DCEPC these are announced in an irregular newsletter named *DC&*. It means DC AND (i.e. DC Additions, Notes and Decisions) which is mailed free to all purchasers of a DDC edition. Since 1997 *DC&* in traditional print form has been discontinued and this newsletter is now available on the Dewey homepage on the internet at http://www.oclc.org. The Dewey Homepage is updated on the first of every month. Therefore, now the DDC users have always an updated DDC. In addition, since 1993 the DDC is also available in CD-ROM format which is published every year with new revisions. However, implementation of changes in library is not as easy, and most of the librarians are scared of it and some hate doing it; some avoid implementing them on one pretext and the other. Only a few libraries implement the new changes; rest continue with the edition once adopted. Bibliographies however use the latest version.

1.3 Salient features of DDC -19(1979)

The 19th edition of the DDC published in 1979 was the last edition edited by able and famous editor Benjamin A Custer (1912-1997), who first edited DDC-16 (1958). The DDC-19 (1979) obviously carried forward the trends of the last three decades, though it did not bring up as many changes as were seen in the DDC-18(1971). The major revision (phoenix schedule) was the new schedule of 301-307 Sociology. Later in 1982 a more detailed version of 301-307 Sociology was issued separately as an independent booklet. Most of the other changes were also in the main class 300 Social sciences. The 329 Practical politics was merged at 324 to form quite a new number, i.e. 324 Political process.

1.4. Changes in tables

There were some changes in the standards subdivisions especially in discontinuation of the ss-08; and an extremely useful Table of Precedence given at the beginning of Table 1. Table of precedence provides standard guidance in case of choice between two standard subdivisions. There was a general 17% increase in the Area Table (Table 2). As a major change the area number of the UK as a whole was shifted to 41 from 42. In fact this change had been in force since 1974.

1.4.1 DDC Manual

A landmark for the DDC practice and standardization came in 1982 with the publication by the Forest Press the *Manual on the Use of the Dewey Decimal Classification, Edition 19* prepared by John P Comaromi and his team. It was a result of a long Survey of the use of DDC in North America conducted by John Comaromi himself in 1975. The Manual explains the DDC perceptions and practices of staff of the Decimal Classification Division of the Library of Congress in applying and interpreting the DDC numbers. It has made possible the uniform application of DDC throughout the world in conformity with the official use. It provides guidance for classifying in difficult areas, and distinguishes one number from other related number. In nutshell the Manual is a blue book on the DDC numbers interpretation and application policies. With many maps, flow charts and detailed point by point elaborations, it is a handy guide for the DDC classifiers for uniformity of applications of the DDC. Because of its success it has been incorporated in the system since the DDC-20 (1989).

1.4.2 Computerization

It is important to mention that DDC-19 was published for the first time through computerized photocomposition. Later from the electronic tapes many path breaking experimental studies were conducted by Karen Markey Drabenstott to study the use of classification (DDC in particular) in online searches and retrieval. Then in 1984 from these tapes a computerised Editorial Support System (ESS) was developed by Inforonics, Inc. for the Forest Press. It started the hitech era for the classification.

1.4.3 Relative index

The relative index continued to be complicated. The only exception was that the bold typeface for entries that were subdivided in the schedules was eliminated.

2. THE DDC-20 (1989)

The 20th edition (1989) brought in many changes which proved to be trend setters. It was edited by a new editor Dr. John P. Comaromi, (1937-1991), a brilliant academician, who had a long time association with DDC in various capacities. Since July 1988 ownership of the Forest Press has been transferred to the OCLC, Dublin, Ohio which started a new era in the development of new DDC products, marketing, research and popularity of the DDC. The system was published in 4 volumes running to 3383 pages compared to 3361 pages in 3 volumes of the DDC-19.

2.1 Editorial Support System

Edition 20 was first to be produced by an online Editorial Support System (ESS) installed by a private company Inforonics, Inc in 1984 in the Decimal Classification Division of the Library of Congress. It is a database of the entire contents of the DDC system and is used to produce future editions and a variety of products. It has almost eliminated the manual/clerical labour in editing and has reduced the production period to six months from the earlier 2 years.

2.2 New Changes

Dr. Comaromi, appointed new editor in 1980, introduced many new changes especially to make the DDC-20 simple, smart and uptodate. It contained many more changes as compared to the previous two editions. Though Comaromi believed in drastic changes to keep pace with growing knowledge, he stuck a diplomatic balance between stability and change. By way of a major development a completely new schedule for 780 Music was incorporated. It had been under revision for the last decade by outside experts. The schedules is not only modern in contents but also more faceted with transparent facet structure. This edition also incorporated 004-006 Data processing and computer science, which was earlier issued as a "separate" between DDC-19 and DDC-20. Minor changes took place in subjects like Christian religion, Television, Adult education, Electronics, Civil rights, Gymnastics and Civil history.

2.2.1 Change in Tables

The new Area table reflected changes in administrative and political setup of different countries and their units. The Table 3 was further refined, modified and split into three subtables: T3A, T3B and T3C. Table 3C is used on instructions from Table 3B or in 808-809 in the Schedules. It has made its application direct and simplified.

2.3 Electronic version

A major achievement of DDC-20 had been its electronic version issued in 1993 on CD-ROM titled *Electronic Dewey.* It contained the DDC-20 Schedules, Tables, Index and Manual as well as the amendments and updatings made in the DDC-20 since its publication in 1989. The disc can be used with a stand alone microcomputer. The Electronic Dewey could be searched by words or phrases, numbers, index terms and Boolean operations. Captions could be browsed and hierarchies could be displayed. An entry also showed frequently used LC subject headings associated with a Dewey number, alongwith a sample bibliographic record. It enabled users to classify materials quickly and efficiently, it was the first CD-ROM version available commercially of any library classification system.

2.4 Simplification Movement

Comaromi will be remembered for his fruitful efforts towards simplification and ease of use of the DDC. Format and presentation of the DDC text was improved in elegance and operation. Namely:

- — Three main summaries were relocated to the second volume.
- — Throughout the schedules and tables many more multilevel

summaries were introduced especially in dense schedules such as 370 Education, 620 Engineering and 630 Agriculture, and also for Area tables of Europe and North America. A multilevel summary is an outline of a class at some lower level, e.g. say outline of 631.11. A multilevel summary allows to view the entire class at one glance, i.e. provides a bird's eye view of that class. It is time saving in locating a number without much scanning and flipping of the schedules pages. It also saves the schedules from physical wear and tear.

— Under each entry detailed definitional and instructional notes have been provided.

— Centered heading were indicated typographically by the symbol ">" in the number column.

— Optional number were given in parenthesis, e.g., (828.9935).

— Manual on the use of the DDC (Forest Press, 1982) was incorporated in the 4th volume (pp. 731-961). Schedules and tables quite frequently referred back to the Manual for further clarification and elaboration.

— As another significant innovation, "Editor's Introduction" was simplified and made simple and brief. It was mentioned : "The introduction is written primarily for the novice or beginning classifiers, although the experienced classifiers may benefit from reviewing its contents" (Introduction, Sec. 1.1).

2.5 Index

Another milestone change occurred in simplifying and trimming the index. It had then been substantially reduced to 730 pages from 1216 of DDC-19. This had been accomplished without impairing its efficiency. All the "See" references had been replaced by direct entries. Synthesised numbers were omitted with a few exception. Terms of the schedules and tables only were indexed. Users convenience and efficiency were the two important achievements of the DDC-20. It was clear, usable and a trend setting edition which was well received by the library world.

3. THE DEWEY-21 (1996)

The 21st edition was released in July 1996, for the first time, simultaneously both in traditional print (in 4 volumes) and CD-ROM forms. Latter is known as *Dewey for Windows (DfW)*. Availability of DDC-20 on CD-ROM facilitated and accelerated the publication of the new edition. By now the relationship of IT and DDC has crossed the teething trouble to enter a mature and fruitful era. As with the earlier edition the editorial work for the DDC-21 was also done on the ESS, now a UNIX based system. As another innovation, members of the DCEPC now hold electronic meetings via the Dewey listserve on the Internet. *DC&* in print form has been discontinued and, instead, is now available on the Internet at http://www.oclc. org/fp. The Dewey Home page also includes the OCLC Forest Press Catalogue , Dewey News, and the 'hot' classification topics and Internet addresses of online catalogues using Dewey. The text in 4 volumes has been edited by a new editor Ms. Joan S Mitchell, appointed Chief Editor in 1993. Ms Mitchell, the ninth editor since Dewey has been associated with the Dewey Organisation since 1985. She is an expert in information technology.

3.1 Structure of the DDC-21

The DDC-21 has the following bibliographic details:

Dewey, Melvil Dewey Decimal Classification and Relative Index/ devised by Melvil Dewey. Ed. 21/edited by Joan S. Mitchell, Julianne Beall, Winton E. Matthews, Jr. and Gregory R. New. Albany, N.Y.: Forest Press a Division of OCLC Online Computer Library Centre, Inc. 1996, 4 Vols. ISBN 0-910568-50-4.

Volume 1 : Prefatory material, Editor's introduction Glossary, Tables 1-7 and information on the changes in the new edition.
Volume 2: Schedules 000-599
Volume 3 : Schedules 600-999
Volume 4: Relative index, Manual

The 4 volumes spread over to 4126 pages have been divided into nine sections marked A/I.

3.2 User's Convenience

The DDC-21 furthers on all aspects the line set by the previous (20th edition) with emphasis on user's convenience and modernisations. Entries are clear with copious notes. Editor's Introduction is brief and simple with improved captions. Many brief manual like notes are also appended to entries in the schedules. Some new types of notes and theoretical concepts have also been introduced.

3.3 Changes in the Schedules

The changes in the DDC-21 are numerous and far reaching in form of additions, expansion, relocations, deletions, and change of heading and newly added notes. The major new schedules are for:

— 296 Judaism and 297 Islam
— 350-354 Public administration
— 368 Insurance
— 370 Education
— 560-570 Life sciences

Some select revisions have been made in 004-006 Data processing, 342-349 branches of laws, 355 Military science, 362-363 Social problems, 420-490 specific languages, 636 Animal husbandry, 790 Theatre, 810-890 Literatures of specific languages, 940-990 General history of the modern world. As an important change in 370 Education, 376 Education of women and 377 Schools of religions have been made subdivisions of 371 education, whereas distance education has been expanded.

3.3.1 Reduction of Bias

A commendable effort has been to reduce Christian bias in religion by shifting Christian religion from 200 to 220/289. Similarly, US bias has been reduced in wording and structure in 350-354 Public administration. It is a big step towards reduction of Western and Christian bias and an effective move towards internationalization.

3.3.2 Changes in Tables

Select changes in the Tables are not less either. Regularisation of standard subdivisions has been carried on bit further. Foremost example is in 370 Education where irregular use of standard subdivision has been replaced by the regular use of T1-07. There has been a regularisation of the use of standard subdivisions at 370.7 and elsewhere in the schedules and related adjustments in T1-071. This brings uniformity and makes the notation mnemonic and faceted. But still more remains to be done, e.g. note the inconsistency below:

340.1 Theories of laws

342.02-.09 Other standard subdivisions of laws

Area table has many significant changes especially in the area table for 47 Russia, 499 Bulgaria. Area numbers for new nations and other geopolitical changes have been incorporated. There are minor changes in other tables.

3.3.3 Transparent Facet Structure

The completely revised schedules (the new edition also avoids the term phoenix schedule adopted in DDC-16/19) not only incorporate new subjects with details but it also provides opportunity to rectify the order of classes and the facet structure to reflect modern thinking in that profession. In the DDC-21 the new schedules have transparent facet structure. It means the DDC is getting more and more faceted. For good or bad the DDC-21 abounds in options in facet formula for local emphasis. For example, in 560-590 Life Sciences the major taxonomic subdivisions have remained the same, but the order of facets has changed from Entity-Process to Process-Entity. Biochemistry from 574.19 has been raised to the status of a section at 572 with ample details and many facets. This is keeping in view the current status of the subject. In 350-354 Public administration. Structure has been improved by reducing US bias. The facet order has been changed from Jurisdiction. Topic to Topic-Jurisdiction. There is also an option here to bring together all topics of Public Administration by area. There are many facet indicators used through many internal tables. Number building has been simplified. For example:

(Public) Administration of Justice in India

353.4 + 09 (Tl) + 54 (T2) = 353.40954 (Option A, Vol. 2, p. 601)

or

351 + 54 (T2) + 0 (Facet indicator) + 34 (from 353.4) = 351.54034

It simply means that the topics of public administration can be collocated by country/place or by topic. In public administration the new numbers are not only shorter but also do away with dual provision of the DDC-20, e.g:

Topic	Ed 20	Ed 21
Abuse of power	351.991 352.002	353.46
Decentralisation	351.0073 352.00472	352.283

3.4 Relative index

Relative index now of 895 pages has been increased by 150 pages due to the addition of many terms and headings. The index includes terms in the headings, and most terms in notes appended with entries in the schedules, and terms in all the seven tables arranged in word by word order. Notes in the *Manual* have also been indexed which lead classifiers to relevant discussion. *See also* references have been employed to draw attention to the broader and related terms. It also indicates the place for the interdisciplinary works in the subject. As in DDC-20, *See* references for synonymous terms have not been used. Instead a term has been indexed under all equivalent terms. For example, Birds and Aves both have been indexed. Under Aves *See also* reference leads to Birds and their all related aspects.

In DDC-21, in accordance with other subjects indexing tools such as Sears List of Subject Headings, and the Library of Congress Subject Headings, uninverted i.e. direct and natural form of phrasal headings have been used. Personal and geographic names have been indexed on AACR-2 specifications. For instance, entry is Civil Engineering, not Engineering, Civil; Commercial art not Art, Commercial.

Some synthesised numbers have been restored in the index based on literary warrants. It incorporates more terms to make it more hospitable to non-US users.

Some concepts and terms implied and some terms obtainable through number building but having sufficient literary warrant have also been included in the index. Apart from physiogeographic names and features, countries and their provinces have also been included in the index. The US geographic details are upto the county level. Some historical events, personalities, kings, queens, eras, names of (literary/social/political) movements have also been included in the index. The index of DDC-21 has best of both the two previous indexes i.e. it has simplicity of DDC-20 and exhaustiveness of DDC- 1 9 indexes. It works smartly.

3.5 Abridged DDC-13 (1997)

First published in 1894 an abridged edition has shorter numbers (normally up to two digits beyond the dot) which are easy to remember and can be easily written on the spine of the document for shelving. Besides this, it is less expensive. In brief it is efficient for a collection upto 20,000 books of a school or public library, and makes a handy tool for teaching DDC.

It is also used in subject headings for children.

Abridged 13 comprising a total of 1026 pages has the following major parts: Prefatory material (pp. i-iii), Four tables (pp. 1-57), Schedules (pp. 59-651).

It is a true abridgement of the DDC-21 (1996) which has been printed from a database prepared at the Library of Congress by a computer assisted Editorial Support System. Abridged 13 subcommittees of ALA Subject Analysis Committee, and (British) Library Association Dewey Decimal Committee have guided the preparation of this edition as they did in case of DDC-21. Accordingly, it has all the new features of the unabridged DDC-21, namely, revised schedules for 350-354 Public administration, 370 Education, 570-590 Life Sciences and new numbers for the countries of the erstwhile Soviet Union among the major revisions. Many notes have been added to provide guidance in use of standard subdivisions in case of multidisciplinary topics. Terminology has been updated to reflect international and current usage; number building instructions have been made explicitly simple. Caption headings have been improved and made more informative. Notes appended to various entries have been simplified and made more comprehensive. Use of standard subdivisions has been bit regularised. It helps in better decision making. There is a long term multi-edition plan to reduce Christian bias. First step has been taken in this edition by shifting the comprehensive number for Christian religion to 230 from 200. In Public Administration, and Life Sciences the citation order of facets have been reversed to reflect the shift in the current literature of these disciplines. *Manual* has been expanded, made more explicit and indexed; and there are more references to the *Manual* in the schedule. In brief the new abridged edition in a single volume provides small libraries the updated features of the unabridged DDC-21 at a much lower price.

3.6 Dewey for Windows (DfW)

The electronics version of DCC-21, named *Dewey for Windows (DfW)* was released simultaneously with the traditional print version in 1996. It is a Microsoft window based LAN compatible version of the Electronic Dewey with DDC-21 database. It provides a window interface which is different from the DOS version of DDC-20 (Electronic Dewey 1993). Search engine in both the cases remains the same. Obviously it requires a micro computer with windows version 3.10 or higher, a 486 based PC or higher with a minimum of 8 MB of memory, a colour monitor with CD-ROM drive. The DfW database began as a database in the Editorial

Support System (ESS) at the Library of Congress. ESS format though different from the MARC format yet there are many similarities between the two. The tapes generated from ESS database are used to produce both the print and CD-ROM format as well as abridged DDC. DfW is updated between editions by issuing a new CD which incorporates changes announced in *DC&* which is now published only on the internet.

Unlike the print editions the CD Dewey is not constrained by the physical size and space. The database includes all built numbers from the relative index of the print version and thousands more added to the electronic version. Each readymade number is accompanied by index terms and the nearest matching DDC schedule number with its verbal heading. It includes the segmentation (prime) marks used by the Library of Congress to show either the end of an abridged number or the beginning of a standard subdivision. A convenient work area displays and stores the parts of the Dewey number being built as one moves among the schedules and tables for instructions.

LC subjects headings have been added to the each class number by statistical matching. These headings provide additional terms for searching. It is an additional help for libraries using LCSH for subject headings, and a source of additional terms for other DfW users. There are some in-built readymade numbers. Keyword access is helpful for finding these already built numbers. Future edition may contain many more such built-in numbers. In DfW movement of upward and downward hierarchies is possible by highlighting and clicking. For interface it uses single function windows. If a number or term is dragged and dropped into a search window, the search for number or the term will begin. For full record display of a number including caption notes, relative index entries and associated LCSH headings of a number that Dewey number is dragged and dropped. If the term is dragged and dropped into an index window set for the relative index the relevant part of the Relative index will be displayed looking like that of the printed relative index.

The windows are arranged in a tiled fashion to facilitate dragging and dropping. There are standard as well as customisable views for the user to set. The standard views are

(a) Search view—search window and DDC number window.
(b) Browse view—search window, DDC pages window and DDC number window.
(c) Scan-view—Index window, Search window, and DDC number window.

(d) Summary view—DDC summary window, Search window, DDC pages window, and DDC number window.

It also provides facility to create i.e. customise our own views to configure the windows to suit ones own approach. The standard views are each described in the Dewey for Windows reference card. As we use the print version of the DDC in different ways i.e. either through the schedules or through the index, so there are different ways to use DfW. Mary Mortimer explains that in any view we can:

— Maximise any window to see a larger display.
— Choose display to see appropriate LCSH.
— Choose bibliographic record to see a sample record using the number selected.
— Change LCSH to review the frequency of headings used with the number
— Contents of a window may be printed by choosing Print.
— Choose Notes to make a permanent record of a DDC number and its specific use.
— Choose Past to review the searches made during the current session.
— Use Help to understand a term or procedure.

It has an augmented index with natural language terms from other thesauri to provide an enhanced access. Some of the important advantages of DfW over the traditional print version are

(a) Keyword access to the entire print DDC-21,
(b) Additional terms for search,
(c) Hierarchic display,
(d) Standard and formulable view,
(e) Dragging and dropping of numbers and terms.

It also remains uptodate without any manual addition from the *DC&* as a new version is issued annually. However the basic principles and number building techniques are the same. Future electronic versions may provide some built-in expert system for automatic synthesis of numbers wherever required. Many surprising features may be in store in the near future including the one Dewey without notation.

3.6.1 Version 2.00 features

This version issued in January 2000 has the following improvements.

— Improved annotation feature is helpful to add as many as 16000 notes to the schedules; can categorise in four different ways and assign a label and multiple keywords for fast and easy retrieval.
— Enhancement to the Dewey for Windows database:
Changes as published in Decimal Classification Additions, Notes and Decisions, vol. 6, Nos 1-3.
— Updated area for France, and the Canadian territory of Nunavut and South Africa.
— An expanded index, including more than 500 built members and accompanying index terms added for popular topics in literature.

For example compare the entry in the indexes of print edition and the DfWs on Computer science:
"Computer science" in DDC21:

Computer science 004
T1-028 5
See Manual at 004-006; also at
004-006 vs. v621.39

"computer science" in Dewey for Windows:
The entries above, *plus:*

Computer science - dictionaries	004.03
Computer science - education	004.071
Computer science - examinations	004.076
Computer science - higher education	004.0711
Computer science - problems	004.076
Computer science - secondary education	004.0712
Computer science - vocational guidance	004.023

As another example Mitchell (2000, p. 85) cites that ecology of Tundras indexed as "Tundras - ecology" in print edition has an additional entry as "Tundra ecology" in the DfW.

— Automatic cuttering, with two options for constructing four-figure cutter numbers.
— New instructions for use of standard period tables for affiliated

literatures.

Any of the following search options can be availed

— Relative index words and phrases
— Captions, words and phrases.
— LCSH words and phrases
— Dewey number
— Basic index of all the fields except LCSH.

4. FUTURE TRENDS

The next edition i.e. DDC-22 is likely to be published in 2003. Joan Mitchell (2000, p. 84) informs that :

> We are investigating major updates in computer science and medicine, continued changes in religion and other updates as needed. We are exploring ways of simplifying number building in literature, an area in which classifiers are often daunted by the complexity of the instructions. We are also considering the deletion of Table 7 (groups of persons) because most of the notation is already available in Table 1 and in the schedules 001-999.

As evinced by the two previous editions the DDC is moving towards internationalization by gradually removing White, Anglo-Saxon and Protestant (WASP) bias. Though able to classify in complex situation it is getting simple to operate. Facet structure is becoming transparent with a capability to hold together many facets in a single class number.

Since the acquisition of the Forest Press by the OCLC Online Computer Library Center, Dublin, Ohio, many innovative efforts have been made to create many Dewey products, such as bookmarks, Dewey rap music, AV teaching kit, Guides to the full, abridged and electronic versions of the DDC, and Dewey posters and exclusive publication of three main summaries. OCLC has sponsored pioneering and successful research to study the use of classification in online databases. Most important of all, research is going on to find wider applications of the DDC in all sorts of information management. Three summaries of the DDC are already being used to organise information on the Internet. For example, a browser based on the DDC has been developed for NetFirst, an OCLC database of source accessible on the internet. Some of the question currently addressed to the DDC are:

— How can the classification be made more effective for classifiers?
— How a standard English language classification be built that also meets the needs of international users?
— How to make DDC more effective in OPACs ?
— How can the classification be made more useful for the end users?
— What can be done to make the Dewey Decimal Classification relevant in the future?

The DDC is geared to become a powerful and reliable subject access system of the 21st century.

REFERENCES

Beall, Jullane, *Dewey for Windows Guide.* Albany, N.Y. : Forest press/OCLC, 1998, 212p. It is also included in the CD version 2.00 and in Help and on the Dewey Web site <www.purl.org/oclc/fp>.

Chan, Lois Mai, *et al.* (1996). *Dewey Decimal Classification: A Practical Guide.* 2nd ed. revised for DDC21, Albany, N.Y. : The Forest Press/OCLC., pp. 1-24.

Chan, Lois Mai and Mitchell, Joan S., Eds., (1997). *Dewey Decimal Classification Edition 21 and International Perspectives.* Albany, N.Y. : Forest Press/OCLC, pp.3-42.

Comaromi; John P. and Satija, M.P. (1990). *Exercises in the 20th Edition of the Dewey Decimal Classification.* New Delhi: Sterling, pp, 127p.

Mitchell, Joan S (1994) "Dewey Behind the Scenes" DC&5 (5) April : 7-11.

Mitchell, Joan S. (2000) "The Dewey Decimal Classification in the twenty first century" In : *The Future of Classification,* ed. by Rita Marcella and Arthur Maltby. Aldershot, UK: Gower, p. 81-92.

Mortimer, Mary (1998). *Learning Dewey Decimal Classification,* Edition 21. Canberra: DocMatrix, pp. 87-88

Satija, M.P. and Comaromi, John, P (1998). *Exercises in the 21st Edition of the Dewey Decimal Classification.* New Delhi: Sterling, 148 p.

Satija, M.P. (1998) "Abridged DDC- 13 and its workbook" *J. Lib & Inf. Sc.* 23(2): 170-173.

INDEX